SPIRITUAL *AND* RELIGIOUS

SPIRITUAL *AND* RELIGIOUS

The gospel in an age of paganism

TOM WRIGHT

First published in Great Britain in 1992
as *New Tasks for a Renewed Church* by
Hodder & Stoughton

This edition published in Great Britain in 2017

Society for Promoting Christian Knowledge
36 Causton Street
London SW1P 4ST
www.spck.org.uk

British Library Cataloguing-in-Publication Data
A catalogue record for this book is available from the British Library

ISBN 978–0–281–07284–2
eBook ISBN 978–0–281–07285–9

Typeset by Lapiz Digital Services
First printed in Great Britain by Ashford Colour Press
Subsequently digitally printed in Great Britain

eBook by Lapiz Digital Services

Produced on paper from sustainable forests

Contents

Preface

The challenges facing today's church often seem insuperable. Those of us who grew up in the UK when churchgoing was still relatively fashionable have watched attendances dwindle, have heard the media laughing at Christians and their beliefs, and have seen Christian values thrown overboard in public life. The same thing has been happening in other parts of the Western world, albeit more slowly in the USA. We know that the church is expanding in the so-called 'developing' countries, but that only makes some commentators sneer at the naivety of such 'unenlightened' societies. In place of an earlier faith, many forms of paganism are now on the rise. It is as well for Christians to be realistic about their present embattled situation.

Two things, however, have to be remembered. First, the early church faced a pagan world far more powerful and entrenched than ours. The gospel of Jesus was born into a world where its central claims were laughed out of court. The message of the crucified Messiah was, as St Paul put it, a scandal to Jews and madness to non-Jews. The wider world was neither expecting nor wanting the kind of 'news' that the early Christians were proclaiming. They already had their own well-developed culture, complete with their own gods and goddesses. Paganism was an entire way of life. Its 'religion' – the worship of the many deities of the ancient world, and the practices that went with that – was simply one way of expressing graphically what human life was supposed to be all about. Our challenges are as nothing to the ones faced by the first Christians. Welcome (they might say) to the normal Christian world.

Second, as the early Christians thought through their faith they saw the death and resurrection of Jesus as the victory of the true God over all the powers of the pagan world. This was paradoxical, to say the least. The pagan world went on persecuting and killing them. But the lived-out message of the gospel made its way none the less. Indeed, the courage of Christians facing torture and death, and above all the love which they showed to one another and even to their persecutors, made people realize that they were embodying a new way of being human. A way which reflected a true God, totally unlike the gods and goddesses the world had known before. So when we go back to the first Christians, and especially the writings of the New Testament, we find a message which fits our own times as much as theirs. If we face a resurgent paganism, we face it with the same assurance of victory as our forebears had.

The present book is written to draw attention to the ways in which various forms of paganism have once again become prominent in our world – and to suggest that, when we look at certain things that have been going on in the church, we don't merely see worrying indications of decline; we see exciting signs that God is doing new things. My overall proposal is that the true and living God has been equipping the church in a variety of ways, ways which seem expressly designed to enable us to meet the new challenges we now face.

One way in which this challenge is often posed can be seen when people say that they are 'not religious', but that they are, in some way, 'spiritual'. By 'not religious' they usually mean that they don't go to church, don't regularly pray, and almost certainly don't read the Bible. But when we look more closely at the way our contemporary world actually works we discover, as we see in this book, that today's society is in fact very 'religious'. The signs of this – the worship of Mammon (the god of money), Aphrodite (the goddess of erotic love), Mars (the god of war or violence) and many other deities – are engrained in the way we think, in the assumptions we make about 'how life works'. When people in this world say they are 'spiritual' what they often mean is that they are aware of 'spiritual' dimensions in their lives (perhaps glimpsed in art or music). There are fewer closed-minded materialists around than there used to be. But the 'spiritualities' of today's world often belong, not with the Jewish or Christian traditions, but with the new paganisms themselves. Today's world is 'spiritual' *and* 'religious', even if both those terms are slippery and easily misunderstood.

The Christian approach to this world, like the early Christian approach to the paganisms of late antiquity, is rooted in the biblical story, focused especially in the story of Jesus himself. The first half of this book therefore follows the double pathway of exploring the world of paganism on the one hand and the story of Israel, with its focus on Jesus and his death and resurrection, on the other. This half of the book follows the journey which many Christians take in Lent each year, starting with Ash Wednesday, a time of reflection and penitence, and moving on to stand at the foot of the cross on Good Friday.

The second half of the book begins with Jesus' victorious resurrection on Easter Sunday. It then works forward, exploring the many new things that God has been doing in the church in recent decades, and suggesting ways in which these movements equip the church for a true, rich spirituality, a 'religion' that goes far beyond the outward shell and into a life-transforming encounter with God and an outward-looking confrontation with the paganisms which corrupt and deface his world. The church from ancient times has celebrated this new way of life in the Sundays following Easter, moving on to the Ascension which sees Jesus enthroned as the true lord of the world (over against all rival divinities), to the gift of the Holy Spirit at Pentecost, and so to the celebration of the life-giving mystery of the Trinity. The second half of the book follows this sequence. The two halves of the book could therefore be used for personal or group studies (for which questions are suggested at the end of each chapter) in the weeks leading up to, and then leading on from, Good Friday and Easter.

This book is a revised version of *New Tasks for a Renewed Church* (in the USA, *Bringing the Church to the World*), originally published in 1992. That book was designed as a gift to the Anglican Diocese of Newcastle upon Tyne in advance of their Diocesan Conference where I was to be one of the main speakers. My prayer now, as then, is that it will help people across the spectrum of Christian faith to glimpse the deeper realities behind today's language of 'spiritual' and 'religious', and to see how the gospel of Jesus enables us to celebrate, and make real in our lives, the new creation which upstages and overthrows all the puffed-up pretensions of paganism.

Tom Wright
St Andrews

Introduction

The train (for once) was early, and stopped on the bridge over the Tyne for a few minutes before pulling in to Newcastle Central Station. I looked out of the window towards the city centre and tried to pick out the familiar landmark of the cathedral among the other buildings. But where was it? It seemed to have disappeared since I was last there. Then I realized. Where I had been expecting the famous lantern tower, all I could see was scaffolding. The cathedral was in the process of having a face-lift. I couldn't see it at that moment, but when it eventually reappeared it would be all the brighter.

Writing about God, the church and the world – in other words, writing theology – can be a bit like erecting scaffolding round a spire. For some of the time, it may seem to obscure the sharp image of the church's witness etched against the secular images all around it. But theology, and biblical study, do not exist for their own sake (though, like a good scaffolder, we theologians sometimes take pride in our work). They exist in order to get the church back into shape for the tasks it needs to perform. There is fabric to be inspected, and some bits need repairing. There are features that ought to be standing out clearly which have been worn smooth by the wind and rain of contemporary thought and pressure. The outline as a whole needs sharpening up. If this book can contribute to the process, I shall be pleased.

The argument I want to advance is quite simple:

1 I believe that our current society presents a new set of challenges to the church. These are significantly different from the challenges that Christians have perceived, and responded to, in recent decades. Fortunately, although these challenges are new to us, they are not totally new in themselves, and we are able to draw on wisdom from the past in addressing them.

2 I believe that the various movements of renewal which have been taking place in the church in the past few decades have been preparing us to meet exactly these challenges. There has been a renewal of Christian interest in ecumenism, in liturgy, in the Holy Spirit, in biblical study, in social and political action, and many other

things. Taken by themselves, these movements can become the hobbyhorses of single-issue fanatics, while the rest of the church wonders what all the fuss is about. But give the church a new sense of direction, a new vision of the challenges that it now faces; show it that, to meet these challenges, it needs to draw on the best that all these renewal movements have to offer; and instead of being the hobbyhorse of a few they become instead the resource-kit of the many. There are new tasks facing us, and a renewed church can face up to them in the knowledge that, through the wise provision of her Lord, she is in principle equal to them.

3 These new tasks for the church demand a new look at, and perhaps understanding of, the question: What is our gospel? It is my firm belief that the answer to this question is found in a new examination of the basic story of Jesus, understanding it within the Jewish context of the time.

Putting these things together, we arrive at the shape of this book. If we are to grasp our present task, we need first of all a clear vision of two entities that at first sight look very different but which in fact have a lot in common.

On the one hand we need to see more clearly what exactly is going on in the modern world, not least the modern Western world. T. S. Eliot, writing in his book *The Idea of a Christian Society* (1939), argued forcefully that societies do not stand still; if they do not embrace a positive ideal (he was advocating the Christian one) they will drift in some other direction. Since Eliot wrote this, we have seen his predictions come true. Those who flatter themselves that they still live in a Christian society today are simply out of touch with reality. We have been drifting towards various sorts of paganism, and it is time to call spades by their proper names.

On the other hand, we need to see more clearly the shape and significance of the central gospel events: the life, death and resurrection of Jesus of Nazareth. Without that we're stuck with a diagnosis and no treatment.

These two things, therefore – analysis of our contemporary culture, and analysis of the gospel events – march side by side through the first half of the book, coming together in Chapters 6 and 7 in a treatment of the cross and resurrection as the divine answer to the plight of the whole world, past, present and future.

The second half of the book applies this more specifically to the details of the present day. If we are to confront the new paganism, we need to worship the true God whose image we are called to bear. Armed with the Bible – and using it responsibly, not as a railway timetable! – we are to address the gods of our day with the news that their time is up. This task cannot be done simply by saying things to one another behind locked doors, and we need to explore some suggestions for hammering it out in practice. If the church is to *be* the church for the world, in any way that makes sense today, it must constantly celebrate and announce the lordship of Jesus in appropriate, constructive and telling ways; and it must do this conscious of the sustaining, humbling and directing power and presence of the Holy Spirit. Ultimately, if the church is to be the church for the world it must recapture a vision of the God who is the true God. This set of issues is our concern in the second half of the book.

I have included a final chapter, as an epilogue, suggesting one particular prayer, and a way of praying it, which picks up the major themes from the book. Some might wish to read this chapter first, and to allow it as it were to pervade and deepen the reading of the rest.

Part 1

THE MODERN WORLD AND
THE CHRISTIAN MESSAGE

1

The kingdom and the church

Announcing the kingdom

It was a hot, sticky afternoon in early summer. I sat in a traffic jam in downtown Montreal, wishing, not for the first time, that the car had air-conditioning. I turned on the radio. A news bulletin slotted itself in between other items. Out in Vancouver a big international exhibition was getting under way. It was the turn of the Russian pavilion to put on its display. There were dignitaries, receptions, speeches. Then, all of a sudden – and this was why it had made the news headlines – a young Jewish man rushed up from the audience and grabbed the microphone. 'I have a message for the Russian people,' he shouted. 'And it's this: there is a God, and he is calling them to account. He will bring them to judgment for . . . ' – but the rest of what he wanted to say was drowned by officials hurriedly snatching back the microphone and bustling him out of the way. I sat there in the traffic jam, listening to the commotion, and the thought struck me with peculiar force: that man was announcing the kingdom of God. Then the second thought: *he doesn't even know the name of the King.*

The ambiguities of his action were plain for all to see. Is that the way to make a protest? Won't it do more harm than good? Surely it's better to work through the normal channels? But the normal channels are just as problematic. And what about the church? Is the church supposed to be standing up and saying something? If so, what? Which microphones should it be grabbing, and what announcement or message should it be getting out before the microphone is snatched back? And, if that young Jew was right in calling the Russian people to repent because of the coming judgment of God, how does his message apply (if at all) to the church or world elsewhere? What ought we to be repenting of, and what difference might it make?

The poignancy of that moment was heightened for me by a second experience, again to do with Vancouver. I was lecturing in the city later that same summer, and had a chance to visit the exhibition. Each country had its own pavilion, displaying different aspects of the national culture. Most striking, to me, were the displays of countries like Pakistan and Saudi Arabia: no sooner did we walk in than we were reminded in symbols and words that these were Islamic countries, running their societies according to the Book, the Qur'an. Everything else was arranged so as to reflect this basic conviction.

And what was the parallel in the pavilions of Western Europe and North America? There was no sign that these countries were (or had been) in any sense 'Christian', except for the odd picture of a cathedral, included as part of the cultural heritage. Instead, what was communicated, as powerfully as the Islamic symbols and words communicated their basic stance, was a commitment on the part of the Western nations to a particular set of cultural symbols: the factory, the industrial complex, the technological innovation. The message came over loud and clear: these countries were basically into the business of making money. Industry and technology were the names of the game, and we were playing it better than anybody else.

And what about the Christian gospel, which used to be, however ambiguously, at the centre of Western culture? Well, at one end of the exhibition site there was a pavilion different from all the others. It was a Christian pavilion. It was attractive, bright, well organized. Inside were books, films, tracts, an amazing variety of presentations and material, inviting people from any nation to find in Jesus Christ that which they could find nowhere else.

Once again I was powerfully struck by a question which has stayed with me, and which is partly responsible for the genesis of this book. Is that really the church's task? Is the church really to sit on the margins of the world, offering a salvation which is an escape, which seems to leave the world to go its own way? Is there no sense in which the gospel has to challenge the central position of technology and business in modern Western society, which has made these the Western equivalent of the Qur'an? Is there no sense, for that matter, in which the gospel has to challenge the central position that the Qur'an itself has in many countries in the world? Is the only purpose of the gospel to offer people a private religious option which, at least at first sight, seems to leave the rest of their lives untouched?

These two vignettes from Vancouver set the scene for the questions we need to address. What are the tasks to which the church is called within society today? How are we to go about grasping them and implementing them? The church, in the Western world at least, has oscillated between two understandings of the task. Are we to leap with both feet into the political pit of snakes, issuing denunciations to left and right, and getting ourselves a bad name for mingling religion and politics, or are we to offer the world a salvation which seems to mean escaping from the world into a private sphere? And, even supposing we could solve this problem at the level of the church's 'official' policy, what does this mean for the ordinary Christian, who carries no political clout and has no particular evangelistic gift?

These are the questions that drive me to reflect, in this first chapter, on repentance, on contrition, on turning away from evil. There is no doubt that something is wrong with our world, and with us as human beings; but what is it that's wrong? How do we go about putting it right? What, in other words, should we be repenting of?

I want to suggest that the church must indeed summon the world to repent, but in a different way from that normally imagined by preachers of either the 'social gospel' of political activism or the 'simple gospel' of personal piety. The modern world is in a crisis of identity. We are like the absent-minded professor who sent a telegram to his wife: 'Am in Coventry. Where should I be?' We have forgotten where we were going. We receive plenty of advice, but whom can we trust? This crisis, I suggest, has produced a state of *paganism* in the modern Western world. That is what the world needs to be told to repent of. This is not how modern Western Christians have normally conceived of their task, and I shall take a little while to spell out what I mean.

In parallel with this, I suggest that the church itself is called, by the same gospel, to repent of its own failures, shortcomings, and folly. Indeed, the church can only really summon the world to repent if it is itself putting its own house in order. This is not to say that we must wait to address the world until we have the church sorted out. We might wait for a long time. Both things have to be done, however imperfectly, at the same time.

I want, therefore, to suggest that at a deep level what matters are the basic assumptions that we make about the way the world is, about what's wrong with it, and about where the solution might be found. People have analysed the world in different ways, and, equally importantly, people who wouldn't be able to articulate such an analysis nevertheless assume it in the way they live. We must look at the two main types of analysis that are offered, and then suggest where they go wrong and what can be done about it. Some people like to cut the world in two. Others like to lump it all untidily together. There are big problems in each way of going about things. If we understand both of them we will have a vital clue to help us through several of the important questions that will occupy us in the rest of this book.

Cutting the world in half

An angry MP writes to *The Times* to complain about a cleric who has 'mixed up religion and politics'. A businessman goes ahead with a money-making scheme despite the constraints of humanitarian ethics. A preacher urges the congregation to leave the worldly concerns of politics and society and discover a 'spiritual' message which is not to be corrupted or compromised by contact with the messy details of political and social life.

In each of these instances, we are seeing a world split in two, with one part labelled 'good' and the other 'bad'. The shorthand word for this is *dualism*. This line of thought goes back to the Greek philosopher Plato. It is still very popular in the Western world, having received a new impetus around three centuries ago through the movement in Western culture known as the Enlightenment. This system divides reality into (a) the world of physical phenomena, and (b) the world of timeless truths, the truths of 'reason'. And it claims that *you can't jump the gap between them*.

It is not difficult to understand why this system, whatever form it takes, is so popular. Humans in general are aware of the contrast between good and evil. They are also aware of the contrast between the material world and non-material values, and can see that some obvious forms of evil are closely associated with the material world. What could be more natural than to identify the two? But this shallow analysis carries all sorts of problems in its wake, as we shall see.

One of the results of dualism is actually atheism. Within much Enlightenment thought, 'God' is a nuisance: he keeps on interfering;

and people who are presuming to speak for 'God' are simply clinging to power for themselves, power which they are using to feather their own nests. So 'God' is (initially) kicked upstairs, and allowed a place, if at all, as an absentee landlord: he may have made the world, and may still take a passing interest in it, but he doesn't do much about it, and we have to get on and fend for ourselves as best we can.

But once you make God an absentee landlord you are half way to making him an absentee. The atheism of Marx and Freud, of Voltaire and John Lennon (who asked us in one of his songs to imagine there was no heaven, saying it would be easy if we tried) is the logical end-product of the absentee-landlord theology, the 'deism', of the eighteenth century. Many in the churches went along with this deism quite happily, since it allowed them to get on quietly with a private or semi-private religion, with no outside interference. A church that has rested content with that compromise has only itself to blame if the world around it regards it as more and more irrelevant. And a good deal of the Western church has not only acquiesced in dualism; it has often mistaken it (as we shall see) for the gospel itself.

But, as G. K. Chesterton remarked, people who give up believing in God don't believe in Nothing. They believe in *Anything*. And Anything has included a large number of alternative systems of belief, some of them bizarre (astrology, fortune-telling and the like); some of them apparently 'normal' and undramatic (materialism, gross national products, and so on); some of them revolutionary (Marxism). We shall look at some of these in Chapters 3 and 5. For the moment, we turn to the mirror image of dualism. Some people are trying hard to put the world all together with no splits at all.

A grand universal theory?

Splits in the world are messy. It is much tidier to hold everything together in one big heap. But how might we do this? Usually it has been done by maintaining the Enlightenment split but arguing that one side is really an aspect of the other. Thus, in the past hundred years, some have tried to argue that everything is reducible to materialism. Everything that *seems* to speak of different dimensions to reality, of a spiritual or transcendent world, is simply the result of social or psychological forces, which can then be reduced to terms of physics, chemistry and biology. Others have tried to argue that the physical world is simply an aspect of the mental world, or perhaps of a great single Mind. If splitting the world in two is called 'dualism', putting it back together again like this is called *monism*.

Of the two sorts of monism just mentioned (Mind-monism and Matter-monism), it is materialistic monism that has ruled unchecked in the Western world for much of recent history. Yet there are huge problems in this way of looking at the world. However hard they may try to be good materialistic monists, most human beings are conscious in some way or other that the world in which they live is not just a place of material objects which can be analysed by scientists, but a place of mystery which invites awe and wonder. The scientist can tell me why a piece of horsehair pulled across pieces of catgut stretched at a certain tension produces a certain note; he cannot tell me why Beethoven's Violin Concerto is so beautiful. The scientist can tell me why the setting sun looks redder than it does for the rest of the day; she cannot tell me why I find the sight of it so evocative. The scientific historian might, in principle, be able to tell me the precise day and hour at which Jesus died; but science in the usual sense will never explain what Bunyan discovered, namely, that the sight of the cross caused his burden to fall off his back. What will the monist make of all this?

The answer is ready to hand in modern Western culture. We must work out a new form of Mind-monism. The modern monist rejects all explanations of the mysteriousness of the world that would take us back to dualism, to the split between the physical world and the non-physical. Rather, in one of the biggest cultural shifts for hundreds of years, we are now living at a time when the material world itself is being looked at with new eyes. It is being invested with the properties that used to be projected on to a reality beyond it: it is the world itself that is God, the One God. Pantheism is the new religion of the masses. There is a great Mind, and it is identified with the world.

Putting the church on the map

At this point someone may express surprise that I have been using abstract terms, without reference to positions that can be explicitly defined as 'Christian' and 'non-Christian'. This is quite deliberate. It is my impression that the majority of Christians in the West hold beliefs about the world, themselves, their god, and their neighbours which may receive 'Christian' labels, but which are in fact simply variations on one or other of the themes I have discussed, none of which are in themselves specifically Christian but are rather part of broad cultural and philosophical strands of development. Where, then, do Christians belong on the cultural map I have been sketching?

Many Christians from a more traditional background are basically dualists. (I am not talking about official theological positions, so much as about the subconscious worldviews of ordinary practising Christians.) They have been taught that the 'world', usually associated strongly with the physicality of creation, is essentially evil; that God sent his Son from beyond the world to rescue us out of it; that (perhaps) God intends to bring the physical world to a well-deserved end, after which we will all finish up either in a non-physical heaven or a non-physical hell.

Those who have grown up with teaching like this, and have been bruised by it, are often the readiest converts to the new monism. They have known in their bones, almost literally, that physicality is not inherently evil, but is a good gift of a loving God; and, after years of attempting to suppress or marginalize their own embodiedness, it comes as a great relief to discover 'creation spirituality'. It offers a new integration, a new wholeness, which the old traditional dualisms had kept at bay.

Somewhere in between the dualists and the monists come the New Theologians of the 1960s (it is always silly to call a movement 'New'), who rejected the old dualism of various fundamentalisms and who went instead for practical or political theology, finding God in the rough and tumble of attempts to carve out a more just and fair society. The theology of the 1960s (one thinks, for instance, of a book like John Robinson's *Honest to God*) looks fairly passé now, but there are still plenty of people around who were brought up on it, and who may now be wondering where to go next.

All of these groups use Christian language; they read Christian texts, particularly the Bible; they practise Christian worship, celebrating the sacraments in one way or another; and they think of themselves, often enough, as the *true* Christians over against the other sorts.

This is where party spirit comes in; and party spirit has been the name of the game in Western Christianity for quite long enough. Many 'evangelicals' are still taught to reject 'liberals' on the grounds that they are 'anti-supernatural'; and, despite old antagonisms, they sometimes team up with catholics of various sorts in defence of 'supernatural religion' against its detractors. But what if the 'natural/supernatural' distinction were itself a legacy from a movement (the Enlightenment) which was not itself particularly Christian, but in fact often specifically anti-Christian?

Equally, many 'liberals' are taught to be afraid of 'evangelicals', on the grounds (for instance) that they hold as certainties things which are not in fact certain, and that they pigeonhole people in unhelpful and dehumanizing ways . . . and the liberal falls into the trap himself, despising 'evangelicals' as being a lesser breed of Christian, and believing quite certainly that we can't know these things for certain. So we could go on.

British culture, in particular, has an unlovely tradition of suspicion and antagonism based on class, region, education and accent; the result is the attitude that says, 'You're different from me, and I resent you for that.' This tendency within our society spills over all too easily into church life, producing divisions that claim to be theological, but which, by making nonsense of so many Christian claims and biblical passages, reveal all too clearly their real nature: they are nothing more nor less than cultural prejudice strutting along in borrowed Christian language. This is not, of course, to say that there are no such things as serious theological debates and divisions; only that a good deal which appears to come under this heading is nothing of the kind. And nothing makes and sustains a 'party' within the church nearly so well as a shared ideology which is in fact not particularly Christian, but which has learnt to use Christian language to give itself legitimacy.

Getting back on track

What are we to make of all this confusion, difficulty and division? The following passages may have something to suggest:

> The kind of fasting I want is this: remove the chains of oppression and the yoke of injustice, and let the oppressed go free.

Share your food with the hungry and open your homes to the homeless poor. Give clothes to those who have nothing to wear, and do not refuse to help your own relatives. Then my favour will shine on you like the morning sun . . . my presence will protect you on every side. (Isaiah 58.6–8, TEV)

'Rend your hearts and not your garments.'
Return to the Lord, your God,
  for he is gracious and merciful,
slow to anger, and abounding in steadfast love,
  and repents of evil . . .

Blow the trumpet in Zion;
  sanctify a fast;
call a solemn assembly;
  gather the people . . .
(Joel 2.13, 15–16, RSV)

But the tax-collector stood a long way off, and didn't even want to raise his eyes to heaven. He beat his breast and said, 'God, be merciful to me, sinner that I am.' Let me tell you, he was the one who went back to his house vindicated by God, not the other. Don't you see? People who exalt themselves will be humbled, and people who humble themselves will be exalted. (Luke 18.13–14)

These passages speak of repentance. Repentance is all about getting back on track, after wandering off in various wrong directions. It involves a serious recognition of personal and collective evil, and a serious determination to behave differently in the future. I suggest that we as a church need to recognize the ways in which we have gone off track, pursuing dualism on the one hand and monism on the other, and to determine, in ways outlined in the rest of this book, to re-order our lives and agendas around the gospel itself.

To the dualist we must say that God's world is an *integrated* whole. The Bible does not envisage a distinction between the physical world on the one hand and the sphere of God's interest and concern on the other. In the Isaiah passage, the prophet is specifically condemning a religious practice that exists simply in a private sphere, unrelated to justice in society. Is he therefore watering down 'spiritual' truth by compromising it with social action? Of course not: 'my favour will shine on you like the morning sun'. God's people are invited – indeed, summoned, – to an *integrated* spirituality.

To the monist we must say that within God's created order two necessary *differentiations* must be made. These are not to be confused with the dualisms we have been discussing. They are:

(a) the proper differentiation *between God and the world*. God is the creator; the world is the creature. They are not the same thing. The creature is made to reflect and indeed be flooded with the glory of God; the world is created good, full of blessing and richness; but God and the world are not the same. We might develop this by pointing out that the world is made good, but *transient*. From the beginning it was subject to change and decay, and the Bible always envisages God as having more in store for his creation than has yet been revealed.

(b) the real differentiation *between good and evil*: between goodness seen as human obedience and its consequences, and evil seen as human rebellion and its consequences. This moral differentiation has nothing to do with being created, or being physical; it has everything to do with the choices we humans make, and their results, for ourselves and for the world.

Dualists characteristically mistake these two for each other. We find it all too easy to imagine that being evil and being physical are bound up together. Conversely, the monist, avoiding this trap, begins by confusing God and the world, and ends by denying the difference between good and evil.

To steer a course between dualism and monism requires a good deal of skill. What we will need, as a church, is a better view of God and the world, a view grounded firmly in the gospel of Jesus and addressed clearly to the situation in which we find ourselves.

Luke's parable of the Pharisee and the publican ought to stand as a dire warning against the phenomenon we have observed, of different religious people using their religiosity as a weapon against one another. It is people like the Pharisee who drive other people into atheism: 'If that's what religion is like,' (we can feel people saying), 'I don't want it.' But the picture of the publican is one which the church could do well to adopt. We have little to be proud of. If we are to make a start at any new tasks – if indeed we are to be renewed at all for those new tasks – then the one thing we must *not* do is to begin them by rubbing our hands with glee at all the wisdom, skill, maturity, insight, knowledge, spirituality, vision or anything else that we already possess, either as individuals or (heaven help us) as parties. That would be to shoot our project in the foot before we'd started. We can only begin with the admission of failure: God have mercy on us, sinners that we are.

We need, then, to repent of our half- and sub- and semi-Christian ideas (dualistic, monistic, or whatever), and of the muddles which have enabled us to imagine we were sound or substantial in our faith when in fact we were half-baked and half-hearted. And we need to repent of having made our muddled and half-grasped theologies into weapons of attack against those we did not like or understand.

If we are to grasp a truer theology it can only be by renouncing, in the manner of a fast, some at least of our old attitudes. Food is good, but we fast in order to learn not to abuse it. Christian doctrinal sensitivity is good, but there may come a time when we have to put it on hold for a while, to check that we aren't abusing it, using 'theological' arguments to support us in battles which have more to do with our cultures, our sub-cultures, our temperaments or our intellectual pride than anything specifically Christian. Let us place ourselves, and our particular theological traditions, firmly in the position of the tax-collector: God have mercy on us, sinners that we are. We are part of the crisis, part of the confusion; let's admit it. Only so may we begin to learn from Jesus himself. And that brings us to our next chapter.

Questions for reflection or group discussion

1 Where does your church stand in the 'theological' spectrum? Are you more inclined to dualism or to monism? Or have you got the balance about right?

2 In what ways do the things your church stands for reflect the things your particular bit of society stands for?

3 Read Isaiah 58.1–8 again. Are there immediate and practical tasks in your local community that would correspond to the things God requires of his people there? How many of them is your church already doing, and how many would it be practical to attempt?

4 In what way is modern Western society failing to heed this same call? Are there ways, in your wider area, in which you could realistically campaign for the alleviation of poverty, homelessness, and injustice?

5 How might you, in your church, integrate those tasks with regular worship?

2

Jesus' world in crisis

If you are the Son of God . . .

We have just seen that the modern world is full of tensions and complexities, not least at the level of analysis itself. But if we think we've got problems, we should try putting ourselves in the shoes of a first-century Jew. Take this one, for example:

> Then Jesus was led out into the wilderness by the spirit to be tested by the devil. He fasted for forty days and forty nights, and at the end of it was famished. Then the tempter approached him.
>
> 'If you really are God's son,' he said, 'tell these stones to become bread!'
>
> 'The Bible says', replied Jesus, 'that it takes more than bread to keep you alive. We live on every word that comes from God's mouth.'
>
> Then the devil took him off to the holy city, and stood him on a pinnacle of the Temple.
>
> 'If you really are God's son,' he said, 'throw yourself down. The Bible does say, after all, that "God will give his angels a command about you"; and "they will carry you in their hands, so that you won't hurt your foot against a stone."'
>
> 'But the Bible also says', replied Jesus, 'that you mustn't put the Lord your God to the test!'
>
> Then the devil took him off again, this time to a very high mountain. There he showed him all the magnificent kingdoms of the world.
>
> 'I'll give the whole lot to you,' he said, 'if you will fall down and worship me.'
>
> 'Get out of it, satan!' replied Jesus. 'The Bible says, "Worship the Lord your God, and serve him alone!"'
>
> Then the devil left him, and angels came and looked after him.
>
> (Matthew 4.1–11)

Jesus' problem is often viewed as a lonely battle between a solitary individual and a cunning demon. But, even though Jesus may have been alone when the battle took place, the point of it was that he was part of a culture in a state of extreme crisis. If we are to understand what his message was, and what it might mean for our own world in crisis, we need to consider the temptations not only of Jesus but of the society of which he was part.

The Jewish world of Jesus' day

To be a Jew in the first century was to live in a time of confusion, conflict, wild dreams, despair and horror. On the one hand, there was social and political chaos; on the other, nationalist hopes cherished with religious zeal. We must look at each in turn.

Political chaos

The Roman overlords never really understood how the Jews thought. They governed with a mixture of provocative folly and crass incompetence. The local puppet rulers, through whom the Romans tried to get things done, were just as bad. Herod the Great, a brilliant upstart three decades earlier, was a morose and malevolent old man at the time of Jesus' birth. When he died there was a flurry of revolutionary movements: now the king is dead, perhaps we Jews can do better for ourselves, and perhaps God will help us! These movements were all put down as Herod's three sons carved up the territory between them. One of these sons is the Herod we meet later in the gospels, with whom John the Baptist came into conflict. One of the others was put in charge of Judaea, but was later deemed incompetent. That was when the Roman governors ('procurators') came in, of whom the best known was Pontius Pilate. In the middle of all this were the local quasi-aristocracy, the chief priests: they held a good deal of power on the local level, but were distrusted and despised by the people as a whole.

On top of all this was the dire financial situation. The problem of debt was acute: Jesus' parables speak of people with debts running into millions, and we may guess that this was something his hearers would have known about. Ordinary people were being taxed out of their wits, and many in consequence were being driven off the land. We in our generation know what happens to a country where people are so desperate that they will do anything for freedom from oppression. We can perhaps enter sympathetically into the Palestine of Jesus' day.

Great expectations

At the same time as all this was going on, Israel clung on to and flaunted the most grandiose expectations any nation had ever held. She believed, in the face of the paganism that surrounded her on every side, that she was the one and only people of the one and only God. Monotheism was not, for a first-century Jew, an abstract or philosophical doctrine, to be debated by scholars. It was a fighting doctrine: it was what you had to believe if you were really committed to the struggle for Israel's national rights. If there was one God only, and this God had made the whole world; and if this God had entered into a solemn and binding pact with your particular people, that you would be his own special people; then either this God was weak and powerless (which was unthinkable) or he must be about to do something to get you out of the mess that you were in. And so the tension between covenant promises and current politics grew more and more acute.

Politics and pressure groups

In the middle of it all there were pressure groups who grabbed the first-century equivalent of the microphone and tried to shout to their fellow Jews that they knew the way forward. There were groups that believed they had been called to go off into the arid wilderness, to band together in communities, to become truly holy through prayer and study of the scriptures, to wait for a deliverance that would come in God's good time, and in the meantime to keep themselves totally unspotted by the world around. One such group, whom we know as the Essenes, was responsible for writing and hiding what we call the Dead Sea Scrolls.

Then there was a group that believed in putting the call to holiness into practice right where people were, making a democratizing attempt to get ordinary Jews practising the details of the law just as if they were themselves priests in the temple. The law, for which their word was Torah, was to apply to the marketplace and the waterfront; to the bedroom and the bathroom; to the kitchen (particularly the kitchen) and the living room. This group held no official position, but exercised an enormous influence over ordinary Jews, who respected their serious scholarship and knowledge of the detail of Torah – which, after all, was the covenant document that Israel's God had made with his people. This group has been much misunderstood by later Christian writers, who read Jesus' and Paul's criticisms of them in the light of later theological controversies. They were called the Pharisees.

One of the Pharisees' main aims was to maintain Israel as the people of God. This was especially important the further one moved away from Judaea, the southern part of the country. (We need to remember that Palestine is about the size of Wales, not the size of the UK, still less of the USA.) In Judaea there was Jerusalem, with its temple. In that region, being Jewish meant going regularly to the temple and participating in the ceremonies. But up in Galilee, seventy miles to the north, things were different. Faced with pagan culture deeply entrenched in their society at every level, the Pharisees emphasized the things that the Jews should do to keep themselves distinct.

This meant two things in particular: keeping the Sabbath, and keeping the food laws. These, together with the mark of circumcision on all male Jews, kept Israel distinct from the surrounding pagan culture and influence. Maintaining these standards was that society's equivalent of flying the Union Jack in a culture where English people are in a minority. It was making a statement. Conversely, those who appeared to go soft on these particular laws would inevitably be seen as traitorous. This had nothing to do with the attitude of petty legalism, whereby one might try to earn God's favour by doing as many moral acts as possible. It had everything to do with a threatened nationalism and its cherished symbols.

There were different emphases within Pharisaism. At one extreme, which we could call left-wing (though such labels can be misleading), the movement shaded off into a different group. Though the word 'Zealot' properly belongs to one group within the great war between the Jews and the Romans in AD 66–70, the modern idea of zealotry, of terrorist groups, bandits, and revolutionary activists, describes well the mood of a good deal of Palestine during Jesus' lifetime. One little group after another banded together, usually around some prophetic or would-be royal figure, and proclaimed that now at last Israel's God was becoming King. There were plenty of Jews in Jesus' day, just as there have been some in our own day, who were announcing to all the world that there was a God who was calling a great empire to account. Their target, of course, was not Russia but Rome. The chief priests were unpopular, and the Herodian dynasty was resented; but, behind both, Rome was the great enemy. It was Rome whose soldiers were trampling the sacred land. It was Rome whose taxes were resented, as much because of their blasphemous coins as because of the hardship they caused.

The great enemies

Rome thus fell heir to a long tradition. Eight centuries before, Assyria had been Israel's enemy, hated and feared. Two centuries after that, it was Babylon. Babylon took the Jews away from their own land, but was then herself overthrown by another nation, Persia. Israel's prophets saw this action as the direct intervention of her God, liberating his people from the results of their sins. If the exile was seen as a punishment for Israel's sins, the end of exile was bound to be seen as the great act which showed that Israel's sins had been dealt with once and for all.

Liberation had occurred, but Israel was still not free! This paradox continued through the succeeding centuries, as different countries ruled Palestine from outside. Matters came to a head in 167 BC: the Syrian megalomaniac king Antiochus Epiphanes carried out his policy of taking over neighbouring states and making them follow his own religion rather than theirs. He took Jerusalem, desecrated the temple, and tortured and killed Jews who resisted. And then the miracle of liberation happened again. A little group, under Judas Maccabaeus, retook Jerusalem and cleansed the temple. It was an extraordinary victory.

For the next two and a half centuries the Jews lived on the memory of that victory, and on the hope which it fuelled: *it could happen again.* When the pagan forces do their worst, our God will act to deliver his people, his city, his holy temple. Folk culture, especially under enemy oppression, has a long memory. In Jesus' own day the legends of the Maccabees were still held up as the shining example of how holy guerrilla warfare can be used by God to defeat paganism.

Symbols of the Jewish world

We can grasp the mood among the Jews of Jesus' day, who stood in this whole tradition, if we consider the symbolism which gave colour and shape to their hope.

The temple

The central symbol was of course the temple itself. It is too easy for readers in the modern West to think of the temple in Jerusalem as the equivalent of a cathedral in a modern city. That is a grave distortion. The temple in Jerusalem was the equivalent (in the case, say, of London) of St Paul's Cathedral and/or Westminster Abbey – but also of the Stock Exchange, the Houses of Parliament, Covent Garden (theatre and market), the butchers' guild, and above all Buckingham Palace. The temple was where the King lived: not an earthly king, but Israel's God. God *was* King; the Jews believed it, whether or not it seemed to be true. And God would *become* King of the whole world, and all would acknowledge him. And the temple was where he had decided, a millennium before at the time of David, to take up permanent residence. The temple was where Jews went to meet with God, to be forgiven, delivered, and restored as his people.

The temple was therefore seen as the focal point of any liberating action which Israel's God would perform on her behalf. It would be rebuilt and renewed as never before (Herod's rebuilding plan, which was going on throughout Jesus' lifetime, made the temple astonishingly beautiful, but few thought that this was really the final rebuilding for which Israel longed). The temple was therefore the greatest of Israel's controlling symbols, drawing together the major themes of her beliefs and hopes.

The land

Jerusalem and its temple were the focal point of the Holy Land. We in the modern West have today almost entirely lost the sense of sacred turf, though several peoples in various continents have not. For the Jews it was (and still is) absolute and non-negotiable. The creator of the world had given Israel his own favourite plot of land, and its very soil was precious. His covenant blessing would rest on its crops, on the flocks and herds that pastured there. To have this land under enemy occupation or rule was not simply resented as a modern Western state would resent enemy occupation. It amounted to blasphemy.

The blessing of the promised land was celebrated in the great agricultural festivals which dominated the Jewish calendar. Most of them were also seen as festivals of liberation. Passover, commemorating the exodus from Egypt; Pentecost, forty days later, commemorating the giving of the Torah as the covenant charter for the redeemed people; Tabernacles, commemorating the wilderness wandering on the way to the promised land; Hanukkah, celebrating the cleansing of the temple by Judas Maccabaeus. These three drew together the symbols of temple and land. The Day of Atonement reminded Jews year by year that, despite their own sinfulness, Israel's God was a forgiving God who would liberate her in the end. Their days of fasting commemorated the destruction of the temple in times past, and thereby looked forward the more eagerly to its final rebuilding and reconstitution when God finally became King. The land would be liberated from foreign oppression.

The law

Torah was taught in the temple, and in the synagogues which sprang up after the scattering of the Jews during the exile. The Torah (the word can be used to denote the first five books of the Bible, or again for what we call the whole Old Testament) was regarded unequivocally as the legal charter which bound God and his people together in a holy covenant. There was no question that obedience to Torah was what constituted Israel as God's people. Disobedience to it, it was widely believed, had caused Israel to go into exile; if her God was still waiting to redeem her, it probably had something to do with her still not keeping Torah as strictly or as accurately as she should be.

Hence the emphasis of the pressure groups, notably the Pharisees: study harder, work out more details, right down to the last jot and tittle – and then maybe God will act. And in the process Torah will keep you separate from the pagans who will always be there to lure you off course. Indeed, when you study Torah *it is as though you are in the temple, in the presence of God*. Torah therefore functioned almost as a portable land, a movable temple: it enabled Jews to worship God truly wherever they were. It thus formed the lynchpin of the Pharisaic movement, seeking as it did to bring the true worship of God right down to the level of ordinary people.

These symbols – temple, land, Torah – thus came together in the great acts of worship, remembrance and hope which formed the grid through which the great majority of Jews of Jesus' day perceived the world. Israel's God was the one true God; Israel was at present suffering at the hands of the pagans; but one day soon God would become King indeed, and then the nations of the earth (particularly Rome) would know who was God, and what this God thought of idols and those who worshipped them. Paganism would be confronted with the sword of the Lord, and the kingdom of God would be established for all time.

The vocation of Jesus

Where did Jesus fit in? It is in this context that we must understand the story of the temptations in the wilderness. They do not simply depict the struggles of an individual searching after holiness and so battling with the flesh, the world and the devil (though they are that as well). They are struggles towards a vocation: what is he supposed to be doing in the present crisis?

It is perilous to attempt to get inside Jesus' mind; but unless we make the effort we will not understand what he was about. We may cautiously reconstruct the situation as follows, remembering that, as with most temptations, the seductive voice may appear to come from a figure outside, but in reality it is heard in what seems like the depths of one's own being.

Jesus was conscious, we may be sure, of a special, vital and living relationship with Israel's God. His cousin John the Baptist had begun a great renewal movement, not entirely unlike other renewal movements at that time and in that area, and Jesus had gone along with it, with a growing conviction that he was to play a crucial role in the liberation of Israel for which everyone longed. He had been baptized by John, in a symbolic act which functioned as a dramatic re-enactment of Israel's leaving Egypt, coming through the Red Sea, and journeying through the wilderness to the promised land – or perhaps a dramatic re-enactment of Israel crossing the Jordan to come and claim the promised land. The symbol of baptism spoke of a penitence which would precede the promised liberation.

Then, as he was baptized, the conviction grew until it burst upon him with a presence like physical form and a voice: *he would be the one through whom Israel's God would accomplish it all.* The awareness of vocation crystallized into a definite, specific and worrying call: 'You are my wonderful son; you make me very glad'. You are (in other words) the one through whom I will do what has to be done. You are the one on whom Israel's fate depends – who will draw Israel's destiny on to himself, and in himself bring it to its glorious climax. You are my son, the Messiah, Israel's anointed king.

Before we proceed, two mistakes in understanding this scene must be warded off. First, it would be quite wrong to imagine that this sense of vocation automatically carried with it the idea that Jesus was therefore 'God incarnate'. Jews of Jesus' day, as we know from various texts, used the phrase 'Son of God' to refer, as does the Old Testament, to Israel, or to her representative, God's anointed. Neither Israel nor the king was thought of as being, in that sense, 'divine'. As on other occasions, we must beware of importing later categories into the discussion. The 'divinity' of Jesus is attested in other and in fact clearer ways, as we shall see.

Second, it would be equally wrong to suppose that believing himself to have heard such a call made Jesus unique among first-century Jews. Not a bit of it. It puts him right in the middle of an already over-crowded map. There were plenty of people, before, during and after Jesus' time, who believed that they were God's chosen and anointed leader, who would liberate his people. One by one they arose, went public, attracted followers, made their bold move, were picked up by the authorities, and were executed. However much Jesus' vocation differed from theirs, to this extent at least the story of his public career is strikingly similar. Nor may we assume that the others were acting in an unreflective or merely impulsive way. They, too, must have thought that Israel's God was calling them to do something special.

So what was Jesus to do? Before him lay a range of options. He could carry on baptizing, working with John (as he seems to have done for a while) to spread the sense of renewal and expectation and to gather more followers around him. He could have taken the path of the Essenes, not far away from where John was working, and collected a community that would keep themselves pure while waiting for God to act. He could have made common cause with the Pharisees, and urged Israel to keep the Torah more perfectly so that then the kingdom would come. Or he could have gathered a group of desperadoes around him, taken to the hills, and planned and prepared for the military or quasi-military revolution towards which Israel's own history, and the expectations of many of her people, were pushing him.

It is in that context that we can understand Jesus' temptations. All around him were siren voices, urging young Jews to act now to bring in the kingdom of God. Perhaps, as we see him confronting the crisis in the Jewish world of his day, we can understand too something of the temptations that face us in our own day, confronting our own world in crisis. What was his vocation to mean for him in practice?

It could have meant abusing his special sense of the providence of God for his own ends. 'If you are God's Son, command these stones to become loaves of bread.' A vocation to service could easily have become an ambition for personal glory and satisfaction. Bread today; servants tomorrow; holding court and dining off gold and silver next week. Against this Jesus set his face. God will provide what his Son needs. In rejecting the possibility of quick satisfaction Jesus is also rejecting the wider possibility that he might blaze a trail of miracles through Israel, providing bread out of nothing for a hungry people, gathering a quick harvest of followers with (presumably) the intention of marching on Jerusalem and being installed as king. What would a kingdom based on feeding miracles look like? It would look suspiciously like the sort of magic trickery that Israel always associated with paganism. It would beat paganism, if it could, by playing it at its own game. It would turn God into a god.

It could have meant forcing God's hand, putting him to the test: this was the second temptation. The Jewish historian Josephus writes of Jews acting precipitately during the war of AD 66–70 in the belief that they could force God into doing something spectacular which would provide a short-cut to victory. But Jesus refuses the route of dramatic compulsion. There can be no short-cuts in God's plan: no neat solutions which bypass the real tasks to be undertaken. You cannot put God in a corner and expect him to act in the way you desire; that would turn God into a mascot, a lucky charm. The second temptation, like the first, is resisted in the name of letting God be God. If Israel is to be liberated, it cannot be on the cheap.

The third temptation is based on the Jewish belief that, when God eventually acted, the nations as a whole would be blessed. Zion (the figurative name for the temple mount) was to be restored, and would then become the highest of the mountains; the nations would flow towards it, coming to hear the word of the Lord and to seek his will and his way (see, e.g., Isaiah 2.2–4). This longing, for a reversal of the present world order in which Israel was trampled underfoot by every foreign nation that cared to try, shaped the culture into which Jesus was born.

Again Jesus is offered a short-cut. There is a present ruler of the world, who claims authority because humans have allowed him to do so (Luke 4.6). The human race as a whole has handed over its God-given responsibility, of being stewards of creation (Genesis 1.28–29, 2.15–19), to a usurper. Humans have refused to take their direction from their creator and, dazzled by the beauty of his creation, have taken their orders from creation instead. In so doing they have unleashed forces which were meant to be kept in their proper place, at the service of humans and creation. And those forces have now claimed the whole world, offering power, prestige, fame, fortune, happiness, honour . . . at a price.

The price is the dehumanization of all who go that route. Worship the creator, and you will reflect his image. Worship forces that arise from within creation (put them all together, and personalize them into 'Satan', if you like), and you will burn brightly for a while before quickly going the way of all flesh. Jesus could have made the ultimate Faustian pact. He refused. Up till now, the temptations had been to use God as a god, or as a mascot. This time, the temptation was to forsake God altogether in favour of a parody-god who would give a cheap imitation of the sovereignty which the Son of God might hope to enjoy – and who would still be the real ruler at the end of the day.

In resisting these possibilities, Jesus was making a deliberate and difficult choice. Relying instead on the scriptures which spoke of Israel's rebellion in the wilderness, prior to her claiming of the land for her God (Deuteronomy 6), he refused to treat God as anything other than God. If he was to speak for Israel and her God, if he was to lead the resistance movement against paganism, he could not go to the task armed with pagan weapons. Like David, he could not take on Goliath with Goliath-like weapons. And it was thus that he came back to Galilee, making the announcement that his contemporaries were longing to hear: God's kingdom is at hand! – but making it in a new tone of voice and with new implications. We began the first chapter of this book with a young Jew announcing the kingdom of God. We end this second chapter in the same way.

Questions for reflection or group discussion

1 Israel's self-understanding was dominated by tales and symbols of God's presence and of liberation. What tales and symbols from our past dominate our self-understanding as a nation and culture?

2 Israel at the time of Jesus was dominated by many competing and/or cooperating powers. Where does real power lie in our society? What resentments arise, as in Israel, because of this?

3 Reflect on each of Jesus' temptations in turn. What would the equivalents be within our society and culture? Which are the easy solutions to the problems we face, which would belittle God and belittle the people who really need help?

4 What then did Jesus mean by going on to announce God's kingdom (Matthew 4.17)? What was the right way forward for him?

5 What would it mean for us to announce the kingdom today? What battles and struggles might we expect, within ourselves and within our society, if we really did it properly?

3

The road to paganism

Substitutes for God

What happens when a society worships something that is not God? We ought to know: it's happening all around us. But we don't usually look at it like that. We live, perhaps, with the delusion that the Western world is still basically 'Christian'; or else we think of our society as simply neutral, an open forum where people can choose their own way forward without pressure from different quarters. We may happen to choose the Christian way; others are free to choose their own.

In this chapter I want to suggest that this simply isn't true, and that one major variety of paganism is so thoroughly embedded in our society that we ignore it as we ignore the mountain that blots out the view from the back window.

If pressed, we would probably agree that things aren't as simple as the picture above. We know about 'the hidden persuaders'; we recognize the insidious power of advertising, of media images, of role models; we know the pressures of popular culture, the desire to be the same (or a little bit better) than the people next door. And yet we fool ourselves that this is merely on the surface, and that underneath lies an ocean of freedom. We reject the determinism that says we are simply the blind servants of psychological forces (Freud) or economic ones (Marx). We can do what we want. We are the masters of our fate.

Pride usually comes before a fall, but in this case it is the fall that came first. The particular blindness which allows this Promethean arrogance to come into being is the result of several generations of Western culture in which God has been banished either to a distant and ineffectual upper chamber or to the sphere of private religious consciousness. We can get on with running the world in a 'neutral' fashion, holding open the religious option should anyone want it, but leaving it out of account when it comes to making real decisions about land, money or human beings. It just gets in the way.

What does religion get in the way *of*? Quite clearly, the other gods that are then being worshipped instead. The rose-tinted picture of a 'neutral' modern Western culture quietly leaves out of consideration the sheer paganism that is now effectively in the driving seat – and the human cost which it exacts. Paganism takes many forms, and it will take us time to examine it.

The nature of idolatry

When Paul went around the Mediterranean world, he encountered human beings enslaved in various ways to the gods and goddesses of paganism. Though we no longer decorate our cities, streets and houses with explicit images of pagan deities, I suggest that our society is as much in bondage to them as was the world to which Paul preached. To see this, we need to understand the nature of idolatry.

Good but not God

Idolatry begins when human beings treat something which is good as if it were God. The world we live in is good, lovely, beautiful; so beautiful, in fact, that it is quite 'natural' to linger and adore it. The world, said the poet Gerard Manley Hopkins, is 'charged with the grandeur of God'. When we look at it, we are meant to find it wonderful, awesome, precious. Not to do so would be to deny the goodness of the creator himself.

It is vital to remember this as we study idolatry. The things to which human beings give mistaken allegiance are not, in and of themselves, bad. The evil consists in human misuse of creation, not in creation itself. When ancient pagans worshipped the sun, they were not making an altogether stupid mistake. The sun is indeed the source of the heat and light that sustains the world. The sun gives great beauty and great blessing to the world. But it is not God. Likewise, when ancient or modern pagans worship the force of sexuality they are not making a merely foolish error. Sexuality is given by the creator as his means whereby species may propagate themselves. Moreover, in its human expression, it is given so that God's own image, male plus female, may celebrate the fact of their image-bearing with a delight and joy which reflects God's own. But, again, sexuality is not God. Thus it is with all idolatry. It is not that the idol is itself bad, only that it is not divine. It is in that spirit that we must approach the task of unmasking, and confronting, the idolatries of which modern paganism consists.

Inflated humanness

Why then do people worship that which is not God? Because it gives them a sense of worth and value. Once I look at something in the material world and cherish it for itself, without reference to the God who made it, and who therefore calls me to a proper sense of responsibility towards it, I am in a dangerous position. My idol gives me a sense of enlargement: I feel more myself when I am with it. I have grown in my own eyes. I am a new person.

A good example of this occurs when someone moves from the innocent enjoyment of belonging to their native country to the idolatrous nationalism which we have seen in so many recent forms. Differentiation between nations and ethnic groups is part of the created order. Enjoyment and appreciation of one's own national identity and characteristics is a perfectly appropriate expression of humanness. But it all too easily passes over into a belief that one's own nation and ethnic group are somehow superior to others.

The alternative is genuine humility when faced with people different from oneself. And genuine humility is hard. It involves letting other people be themselves, without trying to see them as copies or mutations of oneself. The alternative is much easier: to believe in the innate superiority of one's own type of humanness. Idolatry of this sort enables me to feel taller than I really am. The world belongs to me, and I look down on others from a great height. No government tries to curb this sort of inflation.

But what do I have to do to keep my self-inflation up to the mark? I have to go on feeding it. If I feel ten feet tall today, I will want to feel eleven feet tall tomorrow; if I don't, someone will catch me up and overtake me. What I like is the feeling of being a bit taller, and to go on having that feeling I have to have regular doses of inflation . . . which means that I have to find other people to feel superior to. As with all idolatries, if there are people in my way, I may have to walk on a few faces, but that's just too bad. Just don't ask me to shrink to nine feet, let alone eight.

The power of the idol

We may now observe what happens when parts of the good creation become idols. In their proper place, they have a certain power. Nationhood enables human beings to engage in coherent and cohesive common life. Sexuality gives joy and delight, sustains the bond of husband and wife, and propagates the human race. But when these and other things are worshipped in the place of the creator God, they attain a power out of due proportion. Worship your nationhood, and you give nationalism power over you, and over those connected with you, which it should not have. Worship sexuality, and you become its slave, unable to resist its demands, even when they impinge on the freedom and happiness of others.

Idolatry and ideology

Idolatry, once it is well launched, is normally borne along by *ideology*. An ideology is a belief system that sustains, and provides apparently rational legitimation for, the idolatry that is being practised. We can see this, interestingly enough, at the level of language. Nazi Germany produced a whole new vocabulary in which words stood on their heads to mean the opposite of their original sense: 'democracy' meant 'dictatorship', 'freedom' meant 'slavery', and so on. Stalinist Russia did the same. George Orwell, in his book *Nineteen Eighty-Four*, characterized it as Newspeak. This sort of thing is itself a tell-tale sign of what is really going on: language is one of the most precious aspects of our humanness, and when we are prepared to sacrifice it on the altar of our ideologies then we have quietly signed our own death warrants as human beings. We have acquiesced in our own dehumanization.

The process begins with the lie; it continues with the habitual lie; it goes yet deeper when we are unable to distinguish the lie from the truth; and it ends when our words are literally meaningless, the mouthing and mumbling of mechanical untruth that nobody believes but which functions like the clanking of the machinery that says the system is still working. This is the cost of human inflation. We may have felt ten feet tall, but it was a lie. That is the story, in essence, of the Tower of Babel in Genesis 11: humans decide to make themselves taller and taller, but the end result is chaos, confusion, the disintegration of human speech.

The demand for sacrifices

Supposing, then, someone takes away the object of my adoration? Supposing someone else wants to share it with me? Supposing that, in order to give it the attention it seems to demand (if I am to go on receiving from it the sense of self-worth that I enjoy so much), I have to ignore some other demand on my attention which other-wise might have felt quite pressing? Here lies the rub: *idols demand sacrifices*. If I want seriously to worship that which is not God, I must expect that certain things will have to move over and make way for it.

If you want to see this aspect of paganism at work on a grand scale, look again at Nazi Germany. Hitler encouraged the German nation to believe in its own larger-than-life possibilities. Inspired by the phi-losophy of Friedrich Nietzsche (1844–1900), Hitler saw the possibil-ity of creating a race of superhumans. This was exactly the myth that many Germans wanted to believe in, to revitalize themselves after their crushing and demoralizing defeat in the First World War and the difficult years of the Weimar Republic. What stood in their way? The rest of Europe, denying Germany her 'place in the sun'. And, of course, the Jews. They were a different race, a race which, by clearly offering allegiance to a God who could not be assimilated into the German dream, simply didn't fit the pattern. The word 'holocaust' means, literally, a sacrificial burnt offering. Hitler's 'final solution' to the Jewish problem was exactly that: his paganism demanded sacri-fices, and the Jews (among others) were offered on the altar of racial purity.

Of course, we know better now. Or do we? Western society likes feeling ten feet tall. Science and technology have done so much for us: we are better fed, better informed, better equipped, better housed, better entertained than ever before. We are larger than life, and we like it that way.

And who stands in the way of this dream continuing? Some of them live in our midst: the poor, the homeless, those who live in cardboard boxes. Most of us are content to carry on as though they weren't there. Some of them live further away, and we put them out of our minds: the peasant in the Global South who works for a pittance to produce the tea that we buy at inflated prices; the small farmer in a remote village who is entirely controlled by the multinational companies that can put him out of business at the flick of a pen. There is a price to be paid for our idolatry.

The results of idolatry

What happens to those who worship idols? The trouble with idolatry is that it does not give what it promises. It can't. The Psalmist knew this perfectly well:

> Their idols are silver and gold,
>   the work of human hands.
> They have mouths, but do not speak;
>   eyes, but do not see.
> They have ears, but do not hear;
>   noses, but do not smell.
> They have hands, but do not feel;
>   feet, but do not walk;
>   they make no sound in their throat.

And then the devastating conclusion – idolatry breeds dehumanization:

> Those who make them are like them;
>   so are all who trust in them.
>   (Psalm 115.4–8, NRSV)

Why does idolatry mean self-destruction? Because of one of the great truths about being human: *you become like what you worship.* We humans were made in the image of the creator. If we worship him – if, that is, we worship the God revealed in Jesus Christ and by the Spirit – we will begin to resemble him (we may not notice, but others will). Worshipping this God is, in one sense, the 'natural' thing for humans to do; it is what we were made for. And, as he is the author and giver of all life, to worship him is to find our humanness truly enhanced (as opposed to being inflated); to worship him is to discover life, more life, fuller life.

But what if you worship something else? You will be worshipping something in whose image humans are *not* made, and it will start to show. Worship money, power, sex, security, prosperity, political advancement, and it will most likely show on your face sooner or later. It will certainly show in the way you treat yourself, and in the way you treat other human beings. In particular, if you worship some part of the created order, instead of the creator himself, you will be worshipping something that is essentially transient, bound to decay. It does not possess life in and of itself, but only as a gift. But if you begin to bear the image of something that is transient, instead of the life-giving creator, then you are merely reinforcing your own transience: 'those who make them, and trust in them, become like them'. You are choosing decay and death. That is what idolatry produces: the state of being ex-human, a creature that was made to share the glory of the creator but has consistently chosen to worship something else and share its illusory and transient splendour. That is, perhaps, the meaning of hell. Some humans, fairly obviously, arrive there sooner than others.

Out of the maze

So what are we to do about idolatry? How can Western society break out of the deadlock of its ideologies? Two solutions are regularly offered, neither of which is satisfactory.

The first way that seems to lead out of the maze is a programme of stout-hearted renunciation and a determined search for alternative ways of life. We see which idols our society is worshipping; we name them for what they are; and we choose not to worship them any longer. Sounds easy, doesn't it? All we have to do is repent of our folly and blindness and mend our ways. The trouble with gritting our teeth and determining to be better is that, as theologians have observed for many years in relation to individual salvation, you can't pull yourself up by your own bootstraps. As long as we have not addressed the issues in theological terms, seeking the grace of God as the only source of help and drawing on the victory of the gospel itself over all evil, the real idolatries continue unchecked. The church has learnt (though it often forgets again) that individuals cannot be saved by their own moral self-effort, but only through the free grace and love of God, enacted in the cross and through the Spirit.

A second way of addressing the problem of materialistic, post-dualistic paganism is to switch to the more multifaceted paganism of the New Age or one of its satellites. I shall look at this in more detail later, and we need do no more here than notice this as another alternative which, in my view, simply counters one sort of paganism with another.

So how can we move forward out of the maze of the idolatry and ideology that has been characteristic of Western capitalist society? We begin by recognizing that on the cross Jesus won the victory over all opposing powers. We must then confront the idols on their own territory, and must seek to establish the truths of which they are parodies, the true worship of which idol-worship is a distorted image. We must search out the good which is there, and see that it is enhanced, not lost, in the process of abandoning idolatry.

Questions for reflection or group discussion

1 (a) Which idols are regularly worshipped in your local area, and in modern Western society?
   (b) What sort of inflated humanness do they offer?
   (c) What dehumanizing effect do they have on those who worship them, and on other people around?

2 (a) What responses do you, and your church, habitually make to the paganism that you see around you?
   (b) Are these responses effective?
   (c) Do they fully reflect the gospel of Jesus?

3 (a) What ways might there be of celebrating the beauty of the world without worshipping it?
   (b) 1 John 3 speaks of the love of God and of humans. In what way is love the opposite of idolatry?

4

The light of the world

God's answer to paganism

Having looked at paganism in a preliminary way, we must now look at the divine answer to it, as offered in the Old Testament, which is of course the Bible as Jesus knew it. Despite the increasing ignorance of the Old Testament, this strange and powerful old book contains many of the clues to the New Testament and, within that, to the meaning of Jesus' message. We can't assume that we can plunge in to the world of the first century AD and at once understand why people were saying and doing the things they were. We need to understand where they were coming from.

The people of God had begun as a nomadic tribe in the Middle East, about as long before Jesus as we are after Jesus. Their story is told in Genesis 12, and remains foundational to all that Jews and Christians believe. The story of God's good creation, and of human rebellion, as told in the early chapters of Genesis, reaches a climax in Genesis 11, with the story of the Tower of Babel: humans get so over-confident in their own ability that they think they can compete with the creator of the universe. They are wrong. The result is the division of nations and of languages which is symptomatic of the breakdown of relationships between humans in general. Rebellion against the creator results in a fractured world. It is in that context that Genesis tells of a new beginning, a new task, a renewed people.

It begins with one couple. Abraham and Sarah are called to go, with their retinue, to a new land, and to be the spearhead of the creator's mission to his whole world. The whole point of the Abraham story is that it marks the beginning of what God intended to do for the whole creation. But how in the world can a middle-aged Middle Eastern nomad two thousand years before the birth of Jesus be the answer to the problem of the whole world – the problem of human rebellion against the creator, the problem of the fractured nature of human society? People today have difficulty thinking of Jesus himself as the solution to all the problems of the world; how much more so, Abraham. But the answer lies in the question itself: how *in the world?* . . . Many solutions offered to the problems of the world lie essentially *outside* the world. People say, in effect, 'Don't worry about how things are here; there is a different world, and you can escape into it, either by mystical experience here or by passing on from this world into another one.' The solution offered in the Old Testament is quite clearly different. It says: 'Here is a new family; here is a people through whom the rest of the world will be blessed.' This is a people *in the world* and *for the world.* That, and not some other-worldly escapist dream, is what the world needs, and it's what God gave it.

But how does this solution work in practice? It is clearly not going to be a matter of Abraham and his family setting up shop as world-healers and inviting all and sundry to apply to them for good advice. Even if they had tried, they would have been ignored as an internationally insignificant ethnic minority. And it seems that anyway, for quite a bit of the time, Abraham and his family weren't particularly interested in solving the world's problems. They were mostly concerned with staying alive, feeding their flocks and herds, finding fresh pasture, and, later, preserving their national identity. But each time, just when it looked as though the dream was being forgotten, there would arise another member of the clan who could address a fresh word of challenge to the family about the wider task to which it was called. The call to Abraham's family, to be the solution to the problem of the world, is not forgotten, but passed on in hope to the future. As the story of the family unfolds, this hope, and this call, are shaped by three momentous events in particular.

The three great crises

Exodus: priests of creation

The family went through three great crises, each of which (and especially the last) contributed to the way in which Jews in Jesus' day experienced their own version of this sense of vocation. The first was what we call the exodus, the time when God rescued Israel from slavery in Egypt, leading them across the Red Sea and through the wilderness to the promised land. Israel looked back on this as a time when God redeemed her, coming into the slave market (Egypt) and buying a slave (Israel) in order to make her his own special people. 'You are to be for me a nation of priests, a holy nation,' he said (Exodus 19.6). And he gave her a national charter (the law, or 'Torah') which would guarantee that, come what may, Israel would at least have the means available to function as a people who would show the rest of humanity what being human was all about. They were then to build the tabernacle in which the divine presence would dwell, with Aaron and his sons being 'priests' to the 'nation of priests'. This whole picture explains what this 'priesthood' means. If the rest of creation is praising the creator, however inarticulately, Israel was called to gather up those praises and present them, with clear know-ledge and belief, before the creator. Equally, the process was to flow the other way. Israel, having experienced the rescuing power and love of her God, was to be his means of sharing that powerful love with the rest of the world.

Kingship: David and the Holy City

Being a nation of priests is a hard vision to realize, a difficult track to stay on. Faced with the paganism of the ancient world, Israel not surprisingly found it tough to resist the blandishments, the pressure to compromise. Everyone did what was right in his or her own eyes. And in that situation – this is the second great crisis – Israel acquired a king. Should she have done this? Should she have gone on trying to be a theocracy, having no king but God, or should she have a king like all the nations? In one sense, the choice of a king was an act of rebellion against Israel's God; but in another, it was a gift from the loving God to keep his wayward people from going totally astray. This ambiguity is clearly reflected in the texts (1 Samuel 8—12, 15—16, Hosea 13.11, etc.) It looks as though, with hindsight, the Old Testament writers saw *both* that it would have been better if Israel had not needed a king, *and* that, being the people they were, they needed one nevertheless.

Israel's vocation, to be God's means of blessing the world, was then passed on to this king as an individual. In the Psalms (e.g. 2, 21, 72, 89) we find a celebration of the king as the one who will have do-minion over the whole world. This was in part a remembrance of the glorious days under David and Solomon, when the power vacuum in the ancient Near East allowed Israel to expand and rule most of the territory between Egypt and Babylon. The fact that the Psalms went on asserting this sovereignty long after the days of glory had passed away might be seen simply as a bit of patriotic whistling in the dark, keeping up the spirits in times when things weren't so glorious. But it was also a profound restatement of the vision of Abraham and his successors, the vocation that came into focus at the exodus. God will become King over the whole world, not just over Israel; and one of the ways in which this will happen is by his installing a true king, a real second David, in Jerusalem. Then the whole world will be ruled with much-needed justice and perhaps (though not all of the Psalms put it that way) with mercy. We find profound ambiguity in these Old Testament passages: they express, at the same time, a strident nationalism and a true divine vocation to be the means of rescuing the world.

Along with this dream about the king went a dream about Jerusalem. This, too, is shot through with both ambiguity and glory. You could say simply that David had chosen Jerusalem as a shrewd political move, to provide a uniting focus for the twelve separate tribes of Israel. You could point to passages in which Jerusalem is treated almost as a magic symbol, representing Israel's impregnability despite her infidelity. But if David, his capital city, and the temple built by his son Solomon, were the focal political point of Israel, they were also her theological focal point, symbolizing and embodying the promise that through Israel the world would receive the restoration, the reconciliation with the creator, that it so badly needed. The temple was the dwelling place of the creator of the universe. His justice would go forth from Jerusalem, and the word of the Lord from Zion. The nations would come to see that here, and here alone, was true authority, true order, and true healing.

Exile: the vision of renewal

This vision was brutally crushed in 597 BC, more or less half way between the time of David and that of Jesus. The Babylonians came and smashed Jerusalem to bits. The king was taken captive, and his sons killed; so much for the royal family. The temple was destroyed; so much for its being the house of the creator and redeemer God. The people were led into exile; so much for them being the light of the nations.

And yet somehow, astonishingly, hope refused to die. Other nations had had the same treatment and had disappeared without trace. Israel clung to her vision and vocation. Prophets arose to interpret the shocking and horrible events as the inevitable result of Israel's own waywardness and compromise with paganism. The exile did not mean that the creator God had forgotten his people, but that he had remembered them – and that he did not like what he remembered. And if that was the reason, there could be a solution. Israel's God, having abandoned the temple, might one day return. Israel might again be redeemed, might again grasp the vision of being the light of the nations. The nations were still in darkness, and Israel still had, somewhere under layers of her own dark despair, a flicker of hope which might burst again into flame not only for herself but for the nations themselves:

> I am the LORD, I have called you in righteousness.
>   I have taken you by the hand and kept you;
> I have given you as a covenant to the people,
>   a light to the nations,
>   to open the eyes that are blind,
> to bring out the prisoners from the dungeon,
>   from the prison those who sit in darkness.
> I am the LORD, that is my name;
>   my glory I give to no other,
>   nor my praise to idols.
> See, the former things have come to pass,
>   and new things I now declare;
> before they spring forth,
>   I tell you of them.
>
> (Isaiah 42.6–9, NRSV)

Who is being addressed, in this astonishing passage of hope-out-of-despair? On one level, it is clearly Israel as a nation. The whole of Isaiah 40—55 speaks of hope for the nation the other side of exile. But on another level the language is highly individual, addressing Israel as the servant of the Lord, through whom this will be accomplished:

> The Lord GOD has opened my ear,
>   and I was not rebellious,
>   I did not turn backwards.

I gave my back to those who struck me,
> and my cheeks to those who pulled out the beard;
I did not hide my face
> from insult and spitting . . .

He was oppressed, and he was afflicted,
> yet he did not open his mouth;
like a lamb that is led to the slaughter,
> and like a sheep that before its shearers is silent,
> so he did not open his mouth.

> > > (Isaiah 50.5–6, 53.7, NRSV)

Like much of the Old Testament, Isaiah 40—55 contains a profound tension, which the writers of the New Testament subsequently exploit: this 'servant' will accomplish the purposes of God precisely through apparent failure and defeat. But for the moment, the main point is clear. Exile, so far from snuffing out the hope both of Israel and of the nations, will be the springboard for that hope to be realized at last: when Israel herself is finally redeemed from exile, there will follow the great blessing for the world for which Israel was created in the first place. The book of Ezekiel contains an extraordinary and beautiful passage predicting that Jerusalem is to be restored, that the temple is to be rebuilt, and that rivers of living water are to flow out of the temple mountain into all the world, producing healing and new life wherever they go (Ezekiel 47). (This picture is not to be taken literally, as the impossible dimensions of the proposed temple make clear.) The scene is meant to evoke the idea of a restored Eden, with Eden conveniently situated in the Jerusalem temple. Abraham's people will at last be the means of rescuing Adam's tribe from sin, its fatal disease.

These three crises – exodus, the choice of a king, and exile and restoration – provide the wider context within which, as we saw in Chapter 2, the Jewish people of Jesus' day understood themselves and their vocation. These events provided the language, the symbols, and the whole cultural awareness which characterized Jesus' contemporaries.

The Old Testament: the necessary ambiguities

But if the Old Testament sets the scene for Jesus and his contemporaries, it also raises all sorts of puzzling questions. It contains, as we have seen, tensions and ambiguities, which have caused some Christians to back off from all or part of it, feeling somehow that it can't really be 'our' book. There are passages of great and breathtaking beauty, side by side with passages of (what seem to us) horrendous barbarity. And the more strongly we commit ourselves to belief in the inspiration of the Bible, the greater our perplexity. If God really has given us this book, what should we do with it?

The one option that is not open to us is to ignore it. The passages we have examined – Abraham's call (Genesis 12), its renewal at Sinai (Exodus 19), the promise of restoration (Isaiah 40—55), and the vision of Israel's glory and the renewal of creation (Ezekiel 47) – are all picked up in the New Testament, and without them we wouldn't know what was going on within early Christianity itself. One New Testament writer after another echoes the emphasis of Jesus himself: what is happening in the events of the first century is not detached from what went before, but is rather the climax of everything that has passed between Israel and her God up to that point. If we are to understand what Jesus and the New Testament meant by salvation; if we are to understand what the gospel was and is; if we are to understand what the tasks are which the creator God has for his people today, and how he is renewing his church to meet those tasks; then we cannot simply cut the knot and say that we will get by more easily without the Old Testament.

I suggest that we should recognize instead that the Old Testament functions as an earlier act in the great cosmic drama which is still unfolding, and in which we are summoned now to take our own part. It was a necessary act. The drama could not have proceeded without it. It was not, as many Christians have imagined, an unsuccessful first attempt at saving the world which finally had to be abandoned. Nor, however, was it the final and determinative act, which remains for ever static. If we try to summarize the position from a Christian point of view, we might say something like the following.

The creator God desired to work within his own world in order to heal it. No solution imposed from a great height would have done. That would have resulted only in the obliteration of the world by a sweeping declaration of justice, or a totally unjustifiable and immoral wiping of the slate clean in a display of sentimental mercy, with God declaring that humanity's wrong choices didn't really matter, human freedom wasn't really significant, and that all along these human creatures had been puppets, whose strings he could pick up and tweak back into obedience any time he chose. He was therefore bound to work the salvation of the world *from within*; and that meant operating within tension and ambiguity.

Note, I do not say that only Israel, God's people, had to live with ambiguity. It seems to me clear that God himself had to do so. This, indeed, is one of the things that the New Testament writers wrestle with, following the example of Jesus himself. If you commit yourself to helping someone out of a bog in which they are stuck, you can shout good advice from the dry land, but the only way you're actually going to do any good is by going in yourself, getting wet and muddy, and indeed risking getting stuck yourself. Those who think God shouldn't take such risks have a certain logic on their side, but it's a logic which makes nonsense of the Bible, the gospel, Jesus and the Spirit. We may become accustomed to thinking of faith as a risk that *we* have to take. What we don't so easily realize is that it was a risk for God himself – just as much a risk, in fact, as his making a world that was other than himself to begin with.

And that shows us what we're dealing with in the Old Testament: we are observing the results of there being such a God, such a creator, whose very nature is love of such a powerful and creative calibre that it cannot but give itself, pour itself out, into ever new moulds and forms. In the beginning God said 'Let there be . . .', and there was. When humans rebelled, he didn't shut up shop, call in the accounts, and start to play it safe, preferring a logical but loveless existence to the risky enterprise of creation. He took the risk of *new* creation. And the means of this new creation was Israel, herself part of the creation that had rebelled.

God's risk is directly reflected in God's book. As the prophet Ezekiel saw, there was an essential ambiguity even about the holy law itself: God, he said, gave them laws which were not good (Ezekiel 20.25). As Nathan said to David, the real dwelling place of God isn't a building of bricks and mortar, but a human being (2 Samuel 7, compare Acts 7.48). As Jesus himself said, some of the commandments were given because of the hardness of Israel's heart, not because of the permanent will of Almighty God (Mark 10.5). And, as Paul suggests in Romans 4.13, the promise to Abraham that he would inherit one specific piece of territory must be seen in terms of the real divine intention, that the family of Abraham should inherit the entire world. The law, the temple, the land: in each we see the ambiguity which is necessary if the creator is to heal his creation. God had to start somewhere, and he began with one family, one building, one country. The Old Testament reflects that risky but necessary divine decision.

The final ambiguity: Jesus and his mission

But the story of Israel as we find it in the Old Testament is not the end of the drama. As we saw in Chapter 2, the Jews of Jesus' day were longing for the drama to end, believing that its resolution would consist in their eventual liberation from the paganism that still desecrated the sacred land, threatened the holy temple, and prevented a true king from emerging at last to take his place as Israel's rightful and redeeming monarch. They had been promised a bigger and more dramatic return from exile than they had yet experienced: why had it not now come about? And the longer they waited, the more they expressed their hope in purely negative terms: when God acts on Israel's behalf, the nations will be put to rights – by being judged. Israel, called to be the answer to the world's paganism, will provide that answer by simply obliterating it. The world was made for Israel's sake, and when the sons of light fight the sons of darkness there can only be one result.

These were the issues that determined Jesus' announcement of the kingdom of God. Jesus' announcement could so easily have been hijacked by forces on either side. There, waiting for him, were the voices of paganism, of diabolical cunning, urging him to use pagan methods – military might – to defeat paganism. There, waiting for him, were the voices of dualism, suggesting that the kingdom might mean simply a retreat from confrontation with the world and the pursuit of a private religious experience which would allow paganism to keep control of the created order. Jesus refused both routes (though it is sad to see how many people have embraced one or other in his name). Instead, he summoned his fellow countrymen to a new way, a middle way, a different option altogether. Risking (and indeed incurring) misunderstanding on all sides, he urged them to abandon their present way of being Israel, the way of dualistic self-definition over against paganism on the one hand, or cheap assimilation on the other, and to trust him in going a different route, a route that was to lead him into a different sort of confrontation. He would look as though he was losing a battle with paganism, but he would in fact win; and he would win by the only way which would at last shed the long-awaited divine and healing light on to the world.

Jesus and the disciples

How much of all this did the disciples understand? They grasped enough to realize that Jesus was in some sense claiming that Israel's destiny and vocation had devolved on to him. That wasn't a particularly odd thing at the time. Some Jews were looking for a new national leader, and Jesus' agenda could scarcely be articulated without his being seen in that role.

'Who do people say I am?' he asked.

'John the Baptist; Elijah; one of the prophets,' they replied.

That, in itself, tells us something quite important. Jesus was seen by popular contemporary Judaism as a *prophet*; and it was the prophets who had preserved the flicker of light, who had recalled Israel to her vocation to be the light of the nations, at times when it nearly went out altogether.

'But who do you say that I am?'

'You are the Messiah,' Peter responds, voicing the eager and risky enthusiasm of the others, as they talked in revolutionary tones at Caesarea Philippi. 'In you we see Israel's destiny reaching its climax. We will go with you and win the victory.'

Alas for Peter. Jesus, as we shall see, carried in himself all the ambiguities of Israel's destiny: he was to win the victory of life by going to his death. Peter, meanwhile, seems to have embodied all the ambiguities of the Old Testament people of God: he was ready to provide light for the world, even if the light would burn the world to nothing. As Paul said of his contemporaries, Peter had a zeal for God, but without understanding what it was that God was doing (Romans 10.2).

What, then, did the disciples *hear*, as Jesus invited them to follow him to Jerusalem and promised them that the Son of Man would be vindicated after suffering? I think they heard something like this:

'Come with me; we are the little band chosen by Israel's God, as Gideon or Judas Maccabaeus were, in days gone by. We are the ones to fight the crucial battle against the pagans who oppress us from outside, and the traitors who oppress us from within our own ranks. Come with me, and the gates of hell, at present embodied in the wicked regime in Jerusalem, will not stand against us. Come with me, and Judaea will see that Galilee is still faithful to the true God. Come with me; some of us may get hurt, some will even be killed, but we shall win. Our God will see us through. He will vindicate us. And if you draw back, if you are ashamed of me and my agenda, then you will have no part in the vindication which awaits us. Our God is going to set up his kingdom at last; there will at last be no king but God, no Caesar, no Herod – just Israel's God, and his chosen Messiah. This is the generation that will see the final end of exile. Some standing here will not taste death before it all happens.'

That, I think, is what they heard; and they responded. They could not do otherwise. This was the agenda they wanted to hear. This was what faithful Jews had been waiting for. They burnt their bridges and went with him. Is it any wonder that within a short while all they could think of was jostling for positions in the coming kingdom?

But was this what Jesus meant? Did he intend all those nationalist overtones? I think that Jesus, if we may put it like this, faced the same dilemma that God faced during the earlier history of Israel. He had to take the risk. He could not avoid summoning the disciples to follow him to Jerusalem. He knew, I believe, what awaited him there. It was part of the vocation, the strange, redefined messianic vocation, of which we may assume he had long been aware and to which he had pledged specific obedience ever since his baptism. But there was no language available for articulating that vocation that would not be open to the misunderstanding which misted the eyes of the disciples, which distorted their hearing so that they twisted his words into a clear call to nationalist revolt, which left them squabbling about thrones and glory as he went to his own redefined throne of glory, which left them flailing around with swords in Gethsemane while Jesus was fighting a battle with a different enemy. Just as God called Abraham to a vocation which his family would inevitably misunderstand, a vocation to be the light of the nations which could so easily be translated into the vocation to rule the nations from a great height, so Jesus called the disciples to be his right-hand men in a kingdom which they were bound to imagine in nationalist and military terms. If God took the risk of getting his hands dirty when he decided to work with ordinary mortals in order to redeem ordinary mortals, so Jesus took the risk of having his hands pierced with nails when he accepted the vocation to be the heir of Israel's destiny, the light of the world.

His disciples, longing for a leader who would fulfil their dreams, were bound to hear his call to revolutionary love in terms of their own love of revolution. Jesus worked within that misunderstanding. It is just as well that he did. If the creator of the world had waited for a time when people would have understood his desire to save the world, and would have responded without ambiguity to that desire, he would have waited for ever. For such a people even to exist, the great act of salvation needs to come first. This saving act *must* therefore itself take place in a context of ambiguity. It cannot be otherwise. The light must shine in the darkness, even though the darkness does not comprehend it. Therein lies the clue, on the one hand, to a Christian reading of the Old Testament; on the other, to a grasp of what was going on in Jesus' ministry. Israel's vocation, to be the divine answer to paganism, was to be fulfilled. The ambiguities inherent within this vocation were to be embraced by the Messiah himself. They were to lead to the most ambiguous thing God ever did, and the most glorious. But before we reach that point we must look at some further aspects of contemporary paganism.

Questions for reflection or group discussion

1 How do you normally regard the Old Testament and the story of Israel? Which aspects do you find most relevant to you and your church? Which parts do you find most difficult?

2 Why could not God, faced with the rebellion of his human creatures, simply declare a general amnesty – or, alternatively, blot out the entire creation – and begin again from scratch?

3 (a) If Israel, and Jesus' disciples, had to live with difficulties and ambiguities as they struggled to work out their vocation to be the light of the world, what ambiguities must the church necessarily embrace within its own version of the same calling (1 Peter 2.9, Philippians 2.15)? Or has the work of Jesus meant that his followers today no longer need live with any ambiguity?

(b) Peter confessed, with his own agenda in the background, that Jesus was the Messiah. What private agendas today threaten to corrupt the church's confession of faith in Jesus?

(c) Jesus seems to have been prepared to work with the disciples despite their muddled understanding. How much does he require people to believe and grasp today before he is able to work through them? How much does the church as a whole have to grasp correctly before God will use it? What risks are involved?

5

The burning bush

God's strange presence

In one of his most celebrated poems, Gerard Manley Hopkins wrote lines which might almost be a description of the scene as Moses stood before the burning bush:

The world is charged with the grandeur of God.
    It will flame out, like shining from shook foil;
    It gathers to a greatness, like the ooze of oil
Crushed.

('God's grandeur')

We saw in the last chapter that Israel, not least at the time of Moses, was called to be the light of the world. We saw in Chapter 3 that the world has created its own darkness, the darkness of paganism. We must now look at paganism again, only this time the more multidimensional paganism that is making its presence felt particularly in society today. This is not the paganism of materialism. It draws on the other sort of monism, making everything into the expression of a single Mind.

We may begin with Moses. Moses tried to begin a one-man liberation movement on behalf of the Jews in Egypt, and it didn't work. A hasty flight was necessary, and permanent exile looked like being the result. He lived out in the desert, looking after his father-in-law's sheep. But (this pattern will be important later on) his sense that it was wrong for Israel to be slaves in Egypt was not mistaken. God intended to use it, to harness it, to work through it. What he needed was a new vision, a new revelation of God himself. Moses found himself in the presence of a bush that was burning, and yet was not burnt up. And he discovered he was in the presence of the living God.

The burning bush stands as a potent symbol of God in relation to his creation. As in Hopkins' poem, the living God was there, present like fire, present *as* fire, addressing him, warning him that he was standing on holy ground and must take off his shoes at once. Moses was to be commissioned to go back to Egypt, where he had failed before. He was to begin again, this time with the authority of the creator God who chose, on this occasion, to reveal himself in the appropriate symbol of fire. This is not a god who can be reduced to the status of a private cult deity, the property merely of one people. But nor is he a god who can be reduced to a mere nature-god, a feature of the natural order. He is a God who is *present and active within* the natural order, and at the same time *transcendent and beyond* the world he has made.

It is this balance that the human race has always found difficult to maintain in thinking and speaking about God, or for that matter about gods in general. People lurch from thinking of an absent, remote God to thinking of a God who is the sum-total of the various forces of nature. Often they advocate one of these ideas in the mistaken assumption that it is a safeguard against the other. The idea of God being *both* present within his world *and* sovereign over it is not easy to grasp. But it is at the very centre of both Old and New Testaments.

This revelation of the true God results in action. It is a feature of the pantheistic sort of paganism that it leaves the world as it is, and plays down the possibility of human intervention within the world. But when the living God, the creator, addresses his people, he announces that he is going to *do* something, to change the way things are, within his world. What is more, he calls human agents through whom to work. Moses is one of many. There is work to be done which will stretch human responsibility as far as it will go.

The new monism

It is vital that we begin with this picture of the living God, active within his creation, because all around us in contemporary Western society we see movements that have so nearly grasped this truth but have ended up parodying it. Our world is increasingly full of people who are fed up with the prevailing dualisms, and with the one-dimensional materialistic paganism that results from them, and who are moving instead towards conceiving of the world in a different way, sometimes with and sometimes without an explicit theology to back it up.

There are obvious examples. The phenomenon of the city-dweller who decides to sell up and move to the country, giving up busy urban prosperity for the tranquil rural life, has already become a cliché. The remarkable rise in the number of vegans and vegetarians has led fast-food chains to cater for them, something unimaginable a generation ago. A tender conscience about how medicines and make-up are produced, if articulated in the 1950s or 1960s, would have been regarded as cranky. Now, it sounds like common sense. So we could go on. The concrete jungle is cracking up, and new blades of grass are poking their way through into the sunlight. We have heard the call to repent of our exploitation and domination of the natural order, even if not all of us have yet responded as thoroughly as we might. And it would be a foolish or short-sighted Christian who would object to all this.

Along with this wholesome desire to live in harmony with our natural environment, we have taken a new interest in the early history of our countries and ethnic origins. Among some Christians, there has been a revival of interest in Celtic Christianity, the form that the gospel took in the British Isles before the arrival of Augustine of Canterbury from Rome in AD 597. In going back to our roots we feel we are coming closer to an integration of Christian faith and the natural order, instead of embracing a faith that told us to shun not only worldliness but the whole created world. Again, it would be a very odd reaction for Christians to object to such a quest.

But this same trend towards harmony with the natural order and integration with historical roots has other sides to it, which are not so easy to reconcile with mainstream Christianity. Here we must touch on a huge range of movements and phenomena which are all the harder to describe for their being disparate and disorganized.

Sometimes the impetus towards the harmony-with-nature movement has come, not simply from dislike of modern technology and the rat-race, but from a more overt and explicit pantheism, the belief that 'nature' and 'God' are more or less the same thing. (Someone once said to me, in conversation, 'the forces of nature – or what you would mean by "God".' I had to explain that what I meant by 'God' was certainly *not* the same as what was meant by 'the forces of nature', though doing so without lapsing into dualism is never easy, particularly in casual conversation.) There is in contemporary Western society a whole spectrum of belief and practice which comes broadly under this rubric of pantheism.

Most modern pantheists would not belong at either extreme, but might well have a penchant for the idea that our global ecosystem, the world and all that belongs to it, is to be treated like a single organism, and maybe even graced with a personality and a name: 'Gaia' (the word is simply the Greek for 'earth'). This term itself is used in a variety of ways. Sometimes it crops up in serious discussions of ecology, as a convenient shorthand for the total global system to which we belong. At other times the term quite explicitly and intentionally carries the full pagan sense: Gaia is a goddess who must be obeyed, perhaps even worshipped, and who is cross at how her human population have been treating her. Some may use this language simply as a metaphorical way of talking about serious ecology. Others quite clearly intend actual paganism.

This return to harmony with 'nature' (the inverted commas indicate unease: the word 'nature' is regularly used in this connection, but I would prefer to speak of 'creation') is paralleled in its ambiguity by the return to the supposed spiritual roots of our race or nation. In the UK, as we saw, this has sometimes meant a revival of Celtic, or Celtic-style, spirituality. That has often been powerful and enriching. But it has also meant, in other quarters, a return to the pre-Christian religions of Britain: Druidism, for instance, or various forms of witchcraft. This is sometimes paralleled in North America by a romantic hankering after ancient native religions.

It is easy to scoff at the suggestion of such things, and many comfortable middle-class people in the UK and North America go about their lives without any awareness of such activities, except for distant news reports of police being involved in scuffles in cemeteries, or with hooded figures at Stonehenge on Midsummer's Eve. But the phenomenon is increasingly widespread, and its consequences are in some cases very serious. No doubt some of the widely reported cases where sexual and other abuse, in the context of satanic ritual, has been alleged are simply the product of fertile imaginations fed on lurid videos. But there should be little doubt that in some cases abuse does happen. There is such a thing as serious modern neo-paganism, and it has an ugly side as well as a merely quirky one. The practice of witchcraft has been allowed to spread in the Western world because some people choose to believe that it does not exist, while others choose to regard all religious experience, however bizarre, as a private matter which is of no concern to anyone save the practitioner. This attitude is a luxury we can no longer afford.

The Age of Aquarius

At the heart of neo-paganism there stands the nebulous movement known as the New Age. Again I find myself in something of a dilemma in describing this movement. I am aware that some of my readers will never have heard of the New Age, while others will be extremely familiar with it. I cannot here deal with the phenomenon in the depth it deserves; that would take a whole book, and indeed there are plenty available, written from various Christian standpoints. What we can and must do here is give a summary of what the New Age is all about, and of a potential Christian line of comment upon it.

The theory behind New Age thinking, which flourished in the 1980s and 1990s and has continued to affect beliefs and attitudes in the years since then, is fundamentally astrological. The world, we are told, is moving out of the Judaeo-Christian era, which is seen as the Age of Pisces. It is now moving into the New Age, the Age of Aquarius. Those who take this seriously – and they are increasing in number – believe that the transition in question is as important as the Renaissance or the Industrial Revolution, and will see a great change in Western society away from allegiance to the transcendent God of Judaism and Christianity and towards an eastern-style monistic spirituality. Human beings will free themselves of transcendent deities and become conscious of their own inner divinity. This will be the age in which humans achieve a new status. They will become divine.

There are many different phenomena in the current scene which can loosely be summarized under the phrase 'New Age', and many people have been profoundly affected by the movement without actually giving it their explicit allegiance. But at its core the New Age movement has a clear history, a clear ideology, and a definite agenda. Its roots go back at least as far as the atheist philosopher

Schopenhauer, and its pedigree includes the speculative theologian Teilhard de Chardin on the one hand and the composer Richard Wagner on the other. It also has links with influential theosophical and anthroposophical movements of some recent generations. It has given considerable impetus to various movements of modern witchcraft, notably Wiccan practices. In all these respects it is profoundly pagan, profoundly opposed to the traditional meaning of both Judaism and Christianity.

The ideology of the New Age likewise picks up many traditional pagan themes and blends them into one. The world, and all the natural forces within it, consist of the one impersonal divine force which humans are to draw on in order to attain their own full divinity. This can be done by means of special meditation techniques, or by tapping into the power of stone circles and ley lines. The ideology offers a radical alternative to the world-rejecting dualism which has undoubtedly characterized much Christianity. And New Age thinking, as a direct result of its monism, claims again and again to pass beyond good and evil. If I am god, what I want to do is the divine will.

The New Age movement, then, has been important, influential, and widespread. Though it can be seen in all sorts of ways as a healthy corrective to previous dualisms, and particularly to exploitative materialism, it would be naive to think that that is the end of the matter.

Christians and the New Age

How should Christians respond to the New Age movement, and to the whole range of neo-paganisms that cluster around it? Here two things must be said as clearly as possible.

First, we should insist that the Christianity to which neo-paganism and the New Age in particular objects – the Christianity of dualism, of repression, of a great gulf separating God and humans, and humans and the natural world – this sort of Christianity was always unbiblical and unorthodox. The last thing we should do is to retreat into dualism.

Second, though, we must also insist that there can be no compromise between Christianity and paganism. The New Testament is full of the ringing affirmation that Jesus is the only Lord, and when it says Jesus it means Jesus, not a nebulous cosmic Christ who can be reshaped at will. The attempt to integrate worship of the God revealed in Jesus with worship of other gods is not, of course, peculiar to the New Age movement, and mainstream Christianity in every generation has rejected it. This is because to combine Jesus with other gods is to ignore the real Jesus, and so to use Christian language to mean something else. That is what Hitler did in the 1930s, as the leaders of the German Confessing Church pointed out to its cost. The church must be as vigilant as they were in opposing any resurgence of neo-paganism, in whatever 'Christian' guise it may appear.

Various more specific criticisms can be made of the whole neo-pagan movement. But, more seriously, it must be pointed out that the new monism carries a dark dualism at its heart. Its own analysis of evil (always a tricky problem for monists) reduces to this: that there are still many human beings who are living out of tune with the world of nature, out of tune with the god who dwells within them. Indeed, a good deal of human activity is labelled 'bad': technology, and particularly human use of the natural order, is under deep suspicion. But this way of understanding evil is facile and inadequate. It plays down the importance of humanness, the tasks and responsibilities which we all have, in order to play up the supposed goodness and self-sufficiency of the non-human natural order. Against this we must set the Christian doctrine of creation, and of the place and vocation of humans within it. There is such a thing as responsible stewardship, appropriate care and wise use of the created order. To say that we have been unwise and irresponsible is not to say that we should give up stewardship entirely.

The New Age, in short, offers a parody of Christianity, which like all parodies can sometimes look so like the original as to deceive those who had lived for a long time with a different parody, and were getting tired of it. The real cosmic Christ is the one through whom creation was made, the one who now rules as the risen Lord (Colossians 1.15–20); and this is none other than Jesus of Nazareth, the one who died to redeem the world. For Christianity, the real New Age began, not when the world moved on from Pisces to Aquarius, but when Jesus emerged triumphant from the tomb on Easter morning. For Christianity, the destiny which the creator has in store for his human creatures is indeed that they should share his own life; but this will happen not by their discovering 'divinity' within themselves, but by

God's gift of his own Spirit, his own self, to indwell and renew them, making them at the same time fully human, in a way not possible within 'natural', unaided humanity. And the beauty of the world, its strange evocative power and mysteriousness, comes not from the world's being in some sense already divine, but from the fact that it is made *for* God, so that at the end, as the Bible puts it, 'the earth shall be filled with the glory of God, as the waters cover the sea'. What the New Age claims to offer is close to what biblical Christianity offers, even though the church has kept silent about it for so long. But, since it claims to offer it without Jesus, without the cross, and without the Holy Spirit, it can only offer it on the basis of the exaltation and divinization of forces within creation. As we saw two chapters ago, such idolatry leads straight to ruin.

Transfiguration

The story of the transfiguration of Jesus, which occurs at the centre of the first three gospels and is, arguably, diffused all through the fourth, presents a striking and clear Christian viewpoint which affirms all that must be affirmed in the new monistic paganisms while challenging all that must be denied in such movements. The story is well enough known, and picks up from the scene we sketched in the last chapter. Jesus, having been accepted as Messiah by his disciples, has tried to tell them that he must go to Jerusalem, to the cross, and to a strange vindication the other side of death. They have not understood him. A week later, he takes three of them up a mountain, and is suddenly changed in their sight, so that his face and clothes become dazzling, like the sun. He is talking with Moses and Elijah, the great prophetic figures from Judaism's past. And, according to Luke, they are talking about 'his departure [the word in Greek is *exodus*], which he would accomplish at Jerusalem' (Luke 9.31). The disciples, again, cannot understand, and are further terrified when a voice is heard, proclaiming Jesus as God's Son, in words which echo the messianic statements of Psalm 2.7 and Isaiah 42.1. When the vision has passed, Jesus sets his face to go to Jerusalem, where he is to die.

It is vital for our understanding of this story that we do not simply read it as a kind of 'supernatural proof of Jesus' divinity'. The 'divinity' of Jesus is established on quite other grounds. Jesus was not transfigured because he was 'divine'; indeed, the prototype for the shining face within the Bible is Moses himself, in Exodus 34, and it would be a bold commentator who would suggest that Moses was therefore 'divine'. No: the radiance which Jesus possessed visibly on the mountain is the radiance proper to *a human being filled with the glory of God*. Paul speaks of all Christians coming to possess this radiance (2 Corinthians 3.18), and there are several well-authenticated stories of Christians who have experienced something like this. Here we see a vision of the divine destiny for humans, encapsulated in Jesus, the truly human one. And it is Jesus himself, not some not-quite-human Christ, who is thus glorified. It is in Jesus himself, the one authenticated by the transcendent God as the true and only Son, the one greater than Moses and Elijah, that genuine humanness is to be found. And when this true humanness is found it will possess a radiance and a power which will show up all the supposed new consciousness and heightened humanity of the New Age as the borrowed and second-rate thing it is.

In addition, it is vital that we see the transfiguration as a turning-point in the story of Jesus. After his recognition as Messiah, Jesus must go the way of the cross. This is in line with the deep and full analysis of the problem of world evil which was offered in principle in Judaism and brought to its culmination by Jesus himself. Evil is not simply a matter of humans being out of touch with their own inner divinity, and so out of touch with the world. The solution to the problem of evil, therefore, cannot be simply a matter of teaching humans to recognize their own inner nature and to live in accordance with it. Evil is a force to be reckoned with, and the way it is dealt with is by Jesus drawing it on to himself and allowing it to exhaust its power. We will explore this more fully in the next chapter. For the moment, we must grasp the critique of New Age thinking with which the story of Jesus supplies us.

It is the transfigured Jesus who is going to the cross, the one true human being who will give himself, in love, for the world. New Age thinking pursues self-fulfilment; Jesus offers self-forgetfulness. The fulfilment *he* attains is reached on the cross. The claim of Jesus, and of the gospel writers as they tell his story, is this: that, in him, the creator's plan to rescue his world has reached its climax. Israel was called to be God's means of confronting and dealing with the evil in the world; now, in Jesus, Israel has at last been obedient to that vocation. That is why, as we will go on to see, the power of paganism unleashed its full fury upon him. It is also why, in his death and resurrection, he inaugurated the real New Age. The church has forgotten this so often, and has so often taught and lived a watered-down version of it, that it is not surprising that other movements should come in, offering people their own version of the new world which Jesus came to bring about. But with Jesus himself in full view there can be no doubt. For all its grasping of important parts of the truth, the new monistic paganism remains at best a caricature of reality.

Questions for reflection or group discussion

1 What signs have you observed of New Age thinking, or similar phenomena, in your area?

2 (a) What ways might there be of celebrating the goodness of God's creation, and the glory of being human, which avoid idolatry and paganism?
  (b) How might your church help those who have come under the influence of New Age, or other neo-pagan, teaching or practices?

3 (a) Are you aware of witchcraft or other similar practices in your area?
  (b) What, if anything, is the church doing, or should the church do, about it?

6

The other gods were strong

We have now looked, in developing sequence, at the nature of paganism, and at the response to it provided by the creator of the world. We have traced, under this latter theme, God's call to Israel to be the answer to the problem of the world, and Jesus' belief that this call had devolved on to himself. We must now explore the result of that belief, as our two strands or themes come together. It was paganism, human rebellion against the creator and the worship of idols that sent Jesus to the cross. And it was the cross, ironically, that was the ultimate divine answer to paganism.

Confrontation with the powers

When Jesus announced the kingdom of God, he must have known that he was coming into direct conflict with all the power structures around him. To say that Israel's God is King is to imply, quite directly, that Caesar is not. It also implies, nearer home, that Herod is not. More disturbing still for Jesus' Jewish contemporaries, Jesus' redefinition of the kingdom of God clashed directly with virtually all the Jewish expectations. From the outset of his ministry, Jesus seems to have deliberately chosen a course which was bound to lead into confrontation with all the authorities, actual and self-appointed, that exercised power in Palestine.

This wasn't simply a strange death-wish, or a perverse desire, as we see in some demagogues, to be 'agin the government' on every possible point. In a vital passage in St Mark's gospel, we see clearly what the real issues were:

> James and John, Zebedee's sons, came up to him.
>   'Teacher,' they said, 'we want you to grant us whatever we ask.'
>   'What do you want me to do for you?' asked Jesus.
>   'Grant us,' they said, 'that when you're there in all your glory, one of us will sit at your right, and the other at your left.'

'You don't know what you're asking for!' Jesus replied. 'Can you drink the cup I'm going to drink? Can you receive the baptism I'm going to receive?'

'Yes,' they said, 'we can.'

'Well,' said Jesus, 'you will drink the cup I drink; you will receive the baptism I receive. But sitting at my right hand or my left – that's not up to me. It's been assigned already.'

When the other ten disciples heard, they were angry with James and John. Jesus called them to him.

'You know how it is in the pagan nations,' he said. 'Think how their so-called rulers act. They lord it over their subjects. The high and mighty ones boss the rest around. But that's not how it's going to be with you. Anyone who wants to be great among you must become your servant. Anyone who wants to be first must be everyone's slave. Don't you see? The son of man didn't come to be waited on. He came to be the servant, to give his life "as a ransom for many".'   (Mark 10.35–45)

What Jesus was up against, all through his public work, was nothing other than paganism. The way the world organized itself then, as now, was in terms of power, conceived as force, might, superiority, humans lording it over one another. In the ancient world, a glance at the contemporary political scene gives many examples of the phenomenon. The might of Rome, the greatest pagan empire of the day, was built on exactly this foundation. The pagan gods were strong gods, offering to their devotees a like strength. When Rome won a battle, it was the goddess Roma who had triumphed, aided by the battle-god Mars. When Rome became economically stronger, and her citizens so opulent that they wielded the power of the wealthy over those who had less, it was the strong god Mammon who was giving that power to his worshippers. And when Augustus, Tiberius or their successors were honoured and glorified, it was the divine Caesar himself who was in control, ruling the world as only a god could do. Rome, with her empire, was built on the strength of paganism. The situation today is essentially no different.

The tragedy of the Judaism of Jesus' day was the extent to which it, seeing this power, tried to twist its own national vocation and religious heritage into forms which could match it in its own terms. This is what had happened under the Maccabees, two centuries before. This is what would happen a generation after Jesus' death, when various fanatical groups of Jews fought bitterly against the Romans and one another, until Jerusalem finally fell to Titus in AD 70. And this is what Jesus saw, latent even in his own disciples. They were envisaging pagan-style power: Jesus as a new Caesar, Jesus representing Israel's God as a strong god like any self-respecting pagan deity, and themselves as his devotees.

It was this double threat that Jesus resisted. He was offering a radically redefined kingdom of God, and that would include a radically redefined notion of power. Power, he said, comes not in lording it over people but in serving them and, ultimately, in dying for them. Power, as St Paul would later put it, is contained in weakness. This is the ultimate challenge to paganism: a redefinition of power, in which all that paganism boasts of is subverted by a different way of looking at the world altogether.

But this challenge could not simply be encapsulated in a memorable saying, to be handed down and repeated by wondering followers. Jesus' message was first and foremost a programme of action; his words explained the actions he had already performed, and led up to the climactic action he was yet to perform. What were these actions?

The welcome of the outcast

Wherever Jesus went, people who had been pushed to the margins of society suddenly found themselves invited to a party. Jesus regularly celebrated the arrival of the kingdom of God, and there were no bouncers on the door keeping out the undesirables. Indeed, he seems to have gone out of his way to make them welcome, explaining his action in terms of a doctor visiting the sick rather than the healthy. In doing so he was challenging the taboos of his society, according to which Israel was called to purity, and as a result of which many people found themselves permanently ostracized. And he was issuing this challenge in the name of the God of Israel whose kingdom he was announcing and claiming to inaugurate. Somehow, he clearly envisaged his task as being to bring social, as well as physical and spiritual, healing to the people of Israel, and indeed beyond that to the world, and to do so if need be at considerable cost to himself. What could have been in his mind?

Again, wherever Jesus went, people who came into contact with him found a new physical wholeness. This is closely connected with the welcome of the outcast: within the Israel of Jesus' day, many physical ailments disqualified one from full membership in the nation, and some, like the woman with the perpetual haemorrhage in Matthew 9, rendered the sufferer perpetually unclean, with all the social problems and stigmas that this would carry. Jesus' acts of healing, therefore (and there are few serious scholars today who doubt that he did such things), functioned not only as physical healing, but also as social restoration. Jesus comes into contact with illnesses (leprosy, for instance) which would normally be highly contagious; yet rather than the disease clinging to him, he seems instead to have 'infected' the sufferer with a new wholeness. How are we to understand this?

In particular, Jesus seems to have performed a number of exorcisms. Modern readers of the gospels have sometimes been puzzled or embarrassed by these accounts. But they are characteristic of something profound in Jesus' ministry as a whole. Wherever Jesus went, battle was joined. It is as though he and the forces of evil, however we understand them, recognized that they were approaching a final conflict. Why? What was going on?

Jesus and the temple

To answer these questions is to come close to the heart of the Christian gospel, and we must take our courage in our hands and proceed with due caution. There are many answers that might be given, and have been given, to the question of how Jesus understood his own death. What I want to do instead is to explore how the cross functioned, and how Jesus intended it to function, as the great confrontation between himself and the powers of evil. Jesus understood himself to be representing both Israel and Israel's God, and he saw the regimes opposing him, both Roman and Jewish, as representing the powers of evil. Thus, if Israel had been chosen by God to undo evil in his world, and if God himself was active within his world to save it, Jesus was fulfilling both those destinies at the same time. Rome, official Israel, and most of the other actors in the drama, including the muddled disciples, functioned as the representatives of the powers of evil, sending Jesus to the cross – only to find that it turned their world upside down.

We may begin with some important fixed points. First, it seems to me clear that Jesus believed himself to be called to speak and act *as if he were the replacement of the temple and all that it stood for.* If a Jew suffering from impurity wished to be cleansed, he or she would normally go to the temple. If a Jew wished to receive forgiveness of sins, he or she would normally go to the temple. If a Jew wished to celebrate God's restoration of his people, and the hope of a restoration still to come, he or she would normally go to the temple. Throughout his public work, Jesus dispensed cleansing, forgiveness, and the restoration of Israel as though it was his own to give. Though this point is often ignored in both scholarly and popular discourse about Jesus, it seems to me of the utmost significance. Jesus apparently believed that he was called to be and do what the temple was and did.

As we saw in Chapter 4, the temple was the place where Israel's God was supposed to live. If, then, Jesus was claiming to be, as it were, the temple-in-person, he was in that very act confronting the pagan powers of the world with the news: this is where Israel's God is now becoming King! Here is the rallying-point around which the true people of God will gather, so that they may be delivered from the powers of darkness! No wonder the crowds flocked to him. This was what they wanted to hear and experience.

But at the same time his claim was a direct slap in the face to the official cult of the temple itself. If Israel's God really is active in and through Jesus, to forgive, heal and restore his people, then what is to be said about the building which exists to embody that claim? Jesus' answer was brisk: it has become a den of brigands (Mark 11.17), symbolizing that nationalist resistance to Rome which showed that Israel was worshipping a caricature of her own God. Her God was a God of mercy and forgiveness, of healing and restoration; and the temple in Jerusalem was being used as a symbol of military resistance, speaking of a God who wanted to obliterate the world in order to rescue Israel alone. Jesus' agenda was the exact opposite of this. Believing that Israel's destiny had devolved on to him and him alone, he believed that it was his task to be obliterated, in order that the world might be healed.

In order to trace the roots of this belief we would have to look at more passages in the Old Testament, and other Jewish literature, than there is space even to mention here. We might note the strange (and unconsummated) sacrifice of Isaac in Genesis 22. We should certainly note the vocation of Israel, the Servant of the Lord, throughout

Isaiah 40—55 and especially in chapter 53. We should certainly add to the picture, as is done in Mark 10, the image of the Son of Man in Daniel 7, who, apparently as the representative of Israel, suffers at the hands of the 'beasts' and is then vindicated before the transcendent God himself.

An interesting interpretation of this tradition is offered in some later Jewish writings which try to explain the sufferings of the Maccabaean martyrs, two hundred years before Jesus. In books which were well known in Jesus' day, we find such statements as this: through the death of the martyrs, God will vindicate his name against the pagan rulers, and at the same time bring to an end the wrath that has justly fallen on the nation of Israel as a whole (e.g. 2 Maccabees 7.37–38). What is at present preventing Israel from being vindicated against the pagan nations, is her own sin. Divine justice or wrath is in consequence directed against her, and, as so often in the Old Testament, this wrath takes the form of subjugation at the hands of the pagan nations themselves. The achievement of the martyrs is that they should act in Israel's place, as her representatives, taking upon themselves, in their death at pagan hands, the weight of divine wrath which would otherwise fall on the nation as a whole.

This facet of Jewish understanding, I believe, formed a crucial element in Jesus' self-understanding. He would go ahead of the nation, to take upon himself the weight of wrath that would otherwise fall on the people because of their disobedience to their God, because of their idolatry of their own nationhood. For this reason, it becomes clear that his motivation, though parallel in some ways to that of the Maccabaean martyrs, went far beyond that earlier understanding. The other Jewish martyrs saw their death as a means simply of liberating Israel, so that it could again enjoy national sovereignty and hegemony, in a kingdom of God which would also be a kingdom of Israel. For Jesus, his death was to be the means of liberating and blessing the whole world, the whole created order. His welcome to outcasts symbolized a major theme of his entire purpose: Israel was to be the bringer of light for the whole world. The powers of the world, given their spurious authority by the human beings who worshipped them, would be defeated, so that those enslaved to them, like Israel under Pharaoh, would be free from their bondage at last.

This idea of Jesus as the representative of Israel must be seen within the context of Jesus' understanding of himself as the new, or the true, temple. The temple was where Israel's God had promised to meet with his sinful people and, in a daily and yearly repeated miracle, met with them in grace, healing and forgiving them instead of rebuking and punishing them for their sin. Sacrifice is difficult for us to understand today, but we may perhaps see it as the response of total human self-giving to the initiative of total divine self-giving. God gives himself to his people in love, and thus enables humans to come before him with gratitude, bearing as they do so a symbol which speaks both of the costly nature of God's self-giving love and the total self-giving of his people in response. And if Jesus really believed that the role of the temple was now his own role, it makes sense to think that he really did conceive of his own death in sacrificial terms. His death would sum up, in one mighty act, the self-giving love of Israel's God, the creator God, for Israel and for the whole world, and at the same time the vocation of Israel herself, that she should give herself to God's service, even at the supreme cost to herself, as the means of bringing his light to the world.

This helps us to understand, retrospectively, the various actions Jesus was performing during his ministry. He was identifying with sinners and outcasts, so that by apparently becoming a 'sinner' himself actual sinners could be welcomed into God's people. He was allowing the fatal sickness of Israel, and of the world, to infect him, so that his own health might infect them. And, in particular, he was engaging in the climactic battle with the powers of evil that had enslaved not only pagans but also Israel herself. The cross draws together the threads of Jesus' whole public work.

On this basis, I believe, we can both make sense of Jesus' death in the context of first-century Jewish thought-forms and show how that death formed the great and decisive confrontation between Jesus and the pagan powers. (I have written more fully about this in *The Day the Revolution Began.*) Far too often, in my experience, Christians have squabbled over abstract statements of atonement theory, ignoring any consideration of the categories of thought that were available to Jesus himself. Ideas belonging to different thought-worlds have been imported to explain 'how it worked', and controversies have then arisen as to how the details of these alien schemes are to be worked out. But if we begin with the images and ideas readily available to Jesus himself, I believe that the strong points of other schemes will fit within a framework which shows them all to better advantage.

The achievement of the cross

In particular, we can now see how it makes sense to say that, on the cross, Jesus took the weight of the world's evil on to himself. This has often been asserted as an abstract statement of dogma, and equally often challenged by people who are (not unnaturally) puzzled as to why this man's death should be credited with such an odd accomplishment. But, once we grant the initial Jewish assumptions, these questions become reasonably straightforward, albeit infinitely profound.

Israel, we must repeat, believed herself called to be God's agent in the healing of the world. This involved being God's agent in confronting the paganism that was at the heart of the world's problem. We have suggested that Jesus believed this vocation to have devolved on to himself, and acted accordingly. There were two natural reactions to such a ministry. On the one hand, Jews of all sorts were angry at his radical redefinition of their varied ideas of what the kingdom would mean. On the other hand, the pagan Romans themselves were worried lest a potential rival to Caesar should be allowed to escape the normal fate. Together these reactions symbolized and focused the reaction of the whole world, explicitly and implicitly pagan, to Jesus and his dramatic claim. This was simply the climax of the pagan reaction to the whole divine plan, from Abraham to Jesus. To say that the evil of the whole world was heaped on to Jesus on the cross is not simply to deal in theological abstractions. It is to speak of actual historical events.

On the cross, therefore, paganism did its worst. Paganism always seeks to destroy those who oppose its claims, and on Good Friday it looked as though it had scored its greatest success. Once we see the power of evil as a real power, and not merely the hypothetical accumulation of a bundle of small-scale individual sins, the achievement of the cross comes more clearly into focus. Everything that collective human rebellion could become; everything that the radical wickedness of the world could produce; everything that evil powers beyond the range of human comprehension could accomplish; all of that was heaped on to Jesus. And the cross itself, symbol as it is of the worst that paganism can and did do, became also the symbol of the divine victory over that paganism.

Why? Because on the third day Jesus rose again? In a manner, yes. But there is a truth which is to be grasped before even that. By itself, to assert the resurrection as the answer to pagan destruction of Jesus could look as though, after all, Christianity is based on the same sort of power as paganism always claimed. No: the victory of the cross is a victory which was won at the moment of Jesus' death. It was the victory of weakness over strength, the victory of love over hatred. It was the victory that consisted in Jesus' allowing evil to do its worst to him, and never attempting to fight it in its own terms. When the power of evil had made its last possible move, Jesus had still not been beaten by it. He bore the weight of the world's evil to the end, and outlasted it.

It is this great truth that was grasped by the poet Edward Shillito, writing after the First World War:

> The other gods were strong; but Thou wast weak;
> They rode, but Thou didst stumble to a throne;
> But to our wounds only God's wounds can speak,
> And not a god has wounds, but Thou alone.
>
> ('Jesus of the Scars')

The other gods – the pagan pantheon, then and now, and all the local variants on them that appear from time to time – possess power as the world understands power. Jesus did not operate on those terms. He operated on God's terms.

It is at this point, if we are wise, that fear and trembling fall upon us as we contemplate this story. Who is this God? Who is this creator? Who is this, who wins the victory over the evil of the world by dying under its weight? Is this who we mean when we mouth the word 'God'? Do we not at once think of a high-and-mighty being, a God sovereign and majestic, a God who can do what he likes, a tub-thumping, almighty, no-nonsense divine being? How can this God have anything to do with the cross? To answer this vital question we need to take another step back.

The cross, Jesus and God

The Christian claim has always been, at its heart, that we know who the creator of the universe really is when we look at Jesus, particularly when we look at the crucified Jesus. This is such a stupendous and extraordinary claim that it is very difficult to keep it in view. Many people, including many Christians, find it easier to think of 'God' and 'Jesus' in separate compartments, giving lip-service (perhaps) to the idea of Jesus' divinity, but having no idea what it might mean. This is often because people assume that they know the meaning of the word 'God', and then have difficulty fitting Jesus into that meaning. The truth is the other way round. The whole New Testament is written to make the point that, if we will but look at Jesus, we shall discover in a new way who God is.

In concluding this chapter, let us explore this facet of the achievement of the cross. If the cross is the place where paganism becomes most fully itself, demanding the sacrifice of the one who has refused to worship at its shrine, it is also the place where God becomes most fully himself.

We have seen how difficult it is to hold on to a coherent view of God and the world. On the one hand, recognizing evil in the world drives some towards dualism – a view of God and the world with a great gulf between them. On the cross, however, there is no such dualism. God, says St John, so *loved* the world: in Jesus, God and the world meet, and on the cross God takes on to himself the full force of the evil which his creatures have devised. The astonishing truth of the cross is that, faced with his creation in ruins, God does not reject it. He redeems it.

On the other hand, recognizing how good the created world is drives others towards monism – towards a view of God and the world in which the two are almost indistinguishable. From this perspective it is impossible to hold a radical and serious critique of evil, such as the events of the past hundred years or so have shown to be necessary. On the cross, however, such monism is impossible, since the cross shows precisely the radical nature of evil and the even more radical measures that God had to take to deal with it. Faced with the cross, no facile optimism about the world is possible. The cross, therefore, becomes the place where a true Christian view of God and the world gains its proper balance and coherence.

At the same time, the cross becomes the place where paganism's great desire – to find something in the created order which one can worship, from which one will gain strength to be human in a new way – is fulfilled, and so subverted, once and for all. Here at last is a human being, a creature within the world of creatures, who can be worshipped without detracting from the worship of the one true God, but in fact bringing that true worship into proper focus. All idolatry, it seems, is ultimately putting something else in the place – the historic, physical, visible place – that belongs to Jesus alone. The New Testament writers are unanimous in this fundamental claim, even as they are diverse in the manner of its making. It is on the cross that we finally see who Jesus really was all along – and that we finally see who God really was and is all along. Jesus' claim to replace the temple was born out of a belief that he was doing and saying things which were only appropriate for Israel's God, the creator, to do and say. Israel's God had promised that one day he would return in power (as for instance in Isaiah 40.1–11 and 52.7–12), but nobody had known what it might look like when this happened. Jesus appears to have spoken and acted on the assumption that he was embodying Israel's God, coming back at last to rescue his people and the world with the ultimate power, the power of self-giving love. This must always have been a scary, risky belief, held in the knowledge that he, like others, might be deluded. Now, on the cross, the claim is made good. Only the creator of the world can take on the powers of the world and defeat them. As Paul says in Colossians 2, 'He stripped the rulers and authorities of their armour, and displayed them contemptuously to public view, celebrating his triumph over them' (Colossians 2.15).

There are many aspects of the crucifixion which this brief account has not explored. I mention only one, as the crowning glory of all that we have said so far. Paganism thrives on competition, on hatred and anger, on a spuriously inflated humanness which resents any rival, or any diminishing of its own standing. Insofar as Christianity has often betrayed itself into that sort of attitude, it reveals that it has abandoned its point of origin. The genuine article is based on a view of the true God which reveals, above all, his love. The cross is all about a God who loved and who loves; who gave and who gives, gives of himself, gives without measure or backward glance. It is this God whom we are called, as Christians, to worship and serve. It is this God who has won the decisive victory over paganism, and now sends out his people to put this victory into decisive operation.

Questions for reflection or group discussion

1 (a) How does your view of God include the fact of the cross?
   (b) How does God's power show itself in *weakness*? Can you think of examples of this in the modern world?

(c) Jesus enacted the coming kingdom of God by inviting society's outcasts to celebrate with him. How might the church do the same today?

2 (a) How can we hold together the ideas of God's love for the world and God's proper hatred of evil?

3 (a) Jeremiah spoke of a 'new covenant' which God would achieve on behalf of his people (Jeremiah 31.31–34); Jesus spoke of this being fulfilled in his death (Luke 22.20). In what way was this so?

(b) If God defeated paganism on the cross, how does it still have any power from that day on?

7

Jesus' vindication
and the task of the church

We began this book with a young Jew grabbing a microphone and announcing to the world that there was a God. We now come to the point in the story at which, according to the New Testament and Christian tradition, God himself took over the microphone and made some announcements which have changed for ever the course of world history. The whole story is focused in one of the most compact and complex statements of the gospel that St Paul ever wrote:

This is how you should think among yourselves – with the mind that you have because you belong to the Messiah, Jesus:

Who, though in God's form, did not
regard his equality with God
as something he ought to exploit.

Instead, he emptied himself,
and received the form of a slave,
being born in the likeness of humans.

And then, having human appearance,
he humbled himself, and became
obedient even to death,
yes, even the death of the cross.

And so God has greatly exalted him,
and to him in his favour has given
the name which is over all names:

That now at the name of Jesus
every knee within heaven shall bow –
on earth, too, and under the earth;

And every tongue shall confess
That Jesus, Messiah, is Lord
to the glory of God, the father.
                              (Philippians 2.5–11)

This short poetic passage contains a whole wealth of theology, and of practical Christianity. I want to show in this chapter how it draws together the threads of what has been said so far, and how it launches us into the next phase of the story.

Jesus and the story of Israel

One way to understand this passage is to recognize that Paul is telling several stories all at once. On the surface he is, of course, talking about Jesus. He speaks of him as the one who from all eternity was equal to God himself; who became human and died a slave's or rebel's death; and who was then exalted, receiving publicly the rank and title which had always been appropriate for him. But why has Paul said it like this?

One of the most important things about the poem is that Paul is telling the story of Jesus *as if it were the story of Israel.* Whenever Jews tell their story it falls into a recognizable shape, whether they are treating the entire history or one episode within it. Paul picks up all these stories and weaves them together as the story of Jesus.

Take the story of the exodus. Israel was called to be God's people. Then Israel went down into Egypt, and became a slave. God brought Israel up from Egypt and exalted her over the other nations, making her visibly his own people. Israel celebrated this as a great triumph of the true God over the pagan gods.

Or take the story of the exile. Israel was God's people, dwelling in her own land. The Babylonians came and took her away, humbling her before the watching world. The 'exile' was then extended, according to Daniel 9, so that even when some Jews returned from Babylon the pagan nations would continue to rule over them. But Israel believed that her God would rescue her out of this misery, this death, and would vindicate her in the eyes of the nations round about.

The shape of these stories, and of dozens of smaller ones (including those of individuals like Joseph or Daniel), is the same as the shape of the story of Jesus. The difference is that this time the story

71

has involved a *real* death and resurrection. Up to now 'death' and 'resurrection' have been metaphorical. Now they have entered history. What has happened in Jesus is, as it were, the reality towards which the whole story was moving all along. In Jesus, God's plan to act *through* Israel for the world has finally come true. At the same time, God's plan to do *for* Israel what she herself needed has also been fulfilled.

Jesus and the story of humankind

But the passage from Philippians operates also on another level. In Genesis 3, Adam snatched at what he did not possess, namely, equality with God. Paul has told the story of Jesus in such a way as to say: he is what Adam failed to be. He has been the truly human being. He has come to where Adam ended up, to the land of sin and death, in order to rescue and restore humanity.

It is important to notice that this involves a *reaffirmation* of humanness. Many people speak as if humanness were in itself a bad thing. 'I'm only human,' we say, excusing a fault. But in the Bible humanness is essentially a good thing. Indeed, the problem with wickedness, evil and sin is that they corrupt and distort humanness. On the cross Jesus took that corruption and distortion on to himself, its full effects being seen and felt in the horror and agony of the cross. And he dealt with it once and for all. In the resurrection, therefore, there is a joyous reaffirmation of humanness. 'The highest place that heaven affords', that which Jesus is given as he is called 'Lord' in the second half of the poem, is, in biblical terms, the place reserved for the truly human being, not simply for God. This is written into the Psalms which Jesus and Paul knew so well:

> what are human beings that you are mindful of them,
>   mortals that you care for them?
> Yet you have made them a little lower than God,
>   and crowned them with glory and honour.
> You have given them dominion over the works of your hands;
>   you have put all things under their feet.
>
> (Psalm 8.4–6, NRSV)

The lordship which Jesus exercises as the Risen One, he exercises as the true Adam, the truly human being. This, as we shall see, is the basis of God's reaffirmation of the whole created order through the resurrection.

Jesus and the story of God

There is one more level to the story. (Actually, there are several more, but I here focus on the most important one.) Paul, telling the story of Jesus in this poetical fashion, is not content to tell it as the story of Israel and Adam. He tells it as the story of God himself.

We can see this best if we work back from the end of the poem. At the name of Jesus, Paul writes, every knee shall bow. This, again, is a quotation from the Old Testament, this time from the book of Isaiah. In that passage, it is Israel's God who speaks, denouncing the pagan idols as incapable of saving anyone or indeed doing anything creative at all. In one of the most strikingly monotheistic passages of the whole Old Testament, the prophet records God issuing a challenge to the nations, not just to Israel as a whole:

> Turn to me and be saved, all the ends of the earth!
>> For I am God, and there is no other.
> By myself I have sworn,
>> from my mouth has gone forth in righteousness
>> a word that shall not return:
> 'To me every knee shall bow,
>> every tongue shall swear.'
>> (Isaiah 45.22–23, NRSV)

In the resurrection and exaltation of Jesus, Paul sees the establishment of God himself as the sovereign one, the creator of the world, victorious over all his rivals. And he ascribes this glory to *Jesus*. Only a few chapters earlier in Isaiah, God had declared that he would not give his glory to anyone else (42.8). Now, he shares it with Jesus. What has happened? Has God changed his mind? Are there now two Gods? Or has Jesus been swallowed up into God, as it were, like a drop in the ocean?

Paul's revolutionary answer is that the one with whom the living God, the transcendent Father, has shared his glory is the one who always shared it. He was from the beginning 'equal with God'. He was not at that stage human; he *became* human at a particular time and place, without ceasing to be fully God. Indeed, the whole point of the story is that what was done in the humanness of Jesus, and particularly on the cross, was done by God himself. It is precisely because on the cross Jesus did what only God can do that in his resurrection he is exalted to a glory which is God's own unique glory, a glory which Adam was designed to reflect. The story of Jesus is indeed the story of Israel, and of Adam. It is also, if we may put it like this, the human biography of God. The hollow adulation of the crowds on Palm Sunday will give way to the glad affirmation: every tongue shall confess that Jesus, the Messiah, is Lord. In this story we discover the extraordinary truth about the creator of the universe.

Jesus and the confrontation with paganism

The thrust of this remarkable passage in its context is therefore the same as the thrust of the present book. Paul is writing to the church in Philippi, a proud Roman colony full of standard Near Eastern paganism, with a particular allegiance to the imperial cult. Caesar, the mighty emperor over the sea, was hailed as lord and saviour. Paul's triumphant conclusion is not merely a summons to glad worship of this Jesus. It is a deliberate replacement, a dethroning, of the paganism of the surrounding culture. If Jesus is Lord, Caesar is not.

The cross and resurrection thus form, for Paul, the great divine challenge to the pagan idolatry that prevailed all over the Mediterranean world. They are the resource to which he constantly returns throughout his writings. Together they sum up the challenge to paganism that we have seen throughout this book: the call of Israel, the exodus, and the prophecies (not least of Isaiah) about the great victory that the creator God would win over his rivals. It has all come true, says Paul, in the death and resurrection of Jesus.

If, therefore, we are now to consider the church's task in confronting contemporary paganism, we must start with these central gospel events. In the rest of the present chapter I want to suggest that the event of Easter constitutes a fourfold announcement by the creator to his whole world.

Easter and the victory of the cross

First, Easter announces to the world that the cross of Jesus was a victory, not a defeat. Easter transformed the cross, for the disciples, from tragedy to triumph. Instead of being a typical end of a some-what unusual messianic movement, the cross became the sign that this messianic movement had succeeded where all others had failed. Israel's destiny had indeed devolved on to Jesus. This was the shock of Easter, seen from the Jewish perspective. What the Jews expected God to do for them – to vindicate them after their suffering at the hands of the pagans – he had done for Jesus.

The resurrection of Jesus, therefore, functions as the divine proc-lamation to the whole world that evil has in fact been dealt with. There is an inner logic to this that should not be ignored. We saw several chapters ago that idolatry brings ruin: worship that which is not God, that which is not the source of all life, that which is not the being in whose image you were made, and you will end up by ceasing to reflect the true God. Turn aside from genuine humanness, and your humanness will decay and die. In biblical shorthand, the wages of sin is death. Now on the cross, as we have seen, Jesus believed that he was to deal with the evil of the world. How will this be ratified? By his dealing, also, with death. If he has dealt with sin, death can have no hold on him. But if he remains dead, his claim to have dealt with sin is called into question. This is more or less the line of thought Paul follows in 1 Corinthians 15.17–20. This, then, is the first of the Easter announcements: the cross is the decisive victory of the creator God over the evil forces, drawn together as sin and death, that have usurped power in his world.

Easter and the vindication of the creation

Second, if evil has been defeated, what has happened to the created order? In dualistic frames of thought, the evil of the world is so closely identified with creation itself that to defeat evil would mean to abol-ish creation. Some theologies have bought heavily into this scheme, producing a view of the resurrection as essentially a non-physical event (whatever that might be). Evil and physicality are so closely bound up together, for the dualist, that when evil has been dealt with there can be no question of the reaffirmation of physicality. Is that what Easter is all about?

The New Testament is written from a very different perspective. Easter is there seen as the reaffirmation, not the denial, of the goodness of the created order. It is vital to the whole story that what happened on Easter morning was irreducibly physical. This is emphatically not to say that it was a mere return to an ordinary physical human life. If it was anything, it was a going on through death and out the other side to a new sort of life. But – and this is the point – this new life the other side of death *includes* what we think of as 'physicality', even if it transcends it. The life of the resurrection is greater than ordinary mortal human life, but not less physical. The difference between mortal life and resurrection life is like the difference between a telephone conversation and a face-to-face meeting: the latter will still contain the exchange of words, but now in a deeper and richer context. The resurrection reaffirms human physicality, within a context that will make more sense of it, not less.

The resurrection is therefore a triumphant answer to the claims of dualism, repeating the note heard in the first chapter of Genesis: God saw all that he had made, and it was *good*. On Easter morning God looked at his creation, with the power of evil having been dealt the decisive death-blow, and repeated his verdict. And Jesus rose again as the beginning of the new world that is still to come. With the resurrection behind us, it should be impossible for Christians to think of creation other than as the chosen vessel of the creator's love. In the resurrection, God has reaffirmed his commitment to the creation: those who confess their faith in the risen Jesus are not at liberty to regard the world in any other way. The created world is not enemy territory, except by usurping and temporary occupation. It is God's territory, and he has claimed it decisively in Jesus. This is the starting point for all Christian responses to paganism.

The resurrection shows the way to the resolution of a particular puzzle which goes back to the very beginning of creation. We saw, much earlier, that the created order was made good *but transient*. It was not made to be everlasting in its present form. Indeed, part of its quintessential beauty consists in its evanescence, in the fact that we cannot tell the sunset to 'hold it right there', or put the lark's song into a bottle. In the light of the resurrection, we can say with confidence that the whole creation was made to be filled with God's own life and love. When we say, in regular worship, that heaven and earth are full of God's glory, we mean what we say; but they will be filled in a new way at the last, when the work of the Spirit is finally complete. The mistake of paganism is to recognize the beauty of the created order and so to worship it in the present, and for itself, instead of seeing it as beautiful because it is already a reflection of the love and purpose of the creator, and because it will eventually be flooded with his presence.

Easter and the truth about God

Third, if the resurrection thus reaffirms the goodness of the created order, it also reaffirms the claim of the whole Jewish tradition, summed up in the teachings of Jesus: the God who is revealed in the history of Israel is the One God, who has created the whole world. In a post-Enlightenment context, this claim sounds impossibly grandiose. What could possibly vindicate or demonstrate it?

The early church clearly regarded the event of Easter day as such a vindication and demonstration. The context is vital. It was not just anyone who had been raised from the dead. It was the Jesus who had made certain claims, followed a certain programme of action, and brought a whole tradition into focus at one particular point. The resurrection vindicates Jesus, and all that he had said and done. At the same time, the resurrection, though going far beyond anything that had ever happened before, is of a piece with the character of the whole history of Israel, the entire revelation of the Old Testament. But, by being the sort of event it was, it stakes out a claim wider than the traditions and beliefs of just one nation. Death is the great enemy that stalks the whole human race. The resurrection offers itself as the creator's own answer, from within his world.

It is in the light of the resurrection, therefore, that the mainline Christian claims about the meaning of the word 'God' can be made. Who is this God? Easter declares: he is the creator of the universe; he is the rescuer of the universe. He is *both* the transcendent one, beyond all creation, *and* the one who lives within his creation. He has lived a fully human life and died a fully human death within his own world, taking upon himself the pain and shame of the world and exhausting its power. It is in the light of Easter that Thomas, in John 20.28, addresses Jesus in words that are theologically breathtaking even by John's standards: 'My Lord and my God.' From now on, when Christians use the word 'God', that word includes Jesus within its meaning. It is in the light of Jesus that we know who God is.

In particular, in the light of Jesus we know that the true God loves us beyond all telling.

But that is not all. In the same passage in John 20, a little before Thomas' confession, Jesus commissioned the disciples: 'As the Father sent me, so I send you.' Then he breathed on them and said: 'Receive the Holy Spirit.' In the light of John's earlier discussions of the Spirit (chapters 14—16), it should be clear that the Spirit is given as Jesus' *alter ego*. Jesus himself will return to them in a new way, living not merely with them as one human among others, but within them as the source of their life, their motivation, their mission. And this talk of Jesus' Spirit picks up once more all the Old Testament overtones about the Spirit of the living God himself, the transcendent one. This is no new spirit, suddenly invented. This is the Spirit of the living God himself, now known as the Spirit of Jesus. With the achievement of the cross accomplished, the creator can now pour out his Spirit upon all his people, to accomplish his work in his world. Without this full view of God, the task set before the church would not merely be daunting: it would be impossible. With this God, it can be addressed. And this leads to our final section.

Easter and the task of the church

There is a fourth aspect of God's announcement to the world through the resurrection. We have seen that the resurrection of Jesus, while in one sense being the exact fulfilment of all that Israel had hoped for, in another sense took the Jews by surprise. The Jews were expecting the whole nation to be vindicated by God; the resurrection, when it happened, happened to one individual. But there was another unexpected aspect as well. Many Jews had expected that when their vindication came, it would be the end of the whole present mode of world history. Evil would be completely defeated at a stroke; Israel herself would at once be exalted over the nations; the peoples of the world would come to see that her God was indeed God, the creator of the whole world. But when Jesus rose from the dead, history went on as before. Herod and Pilate were still ruling Palestine. Caesar was still on his throne. Nothing seemed to have changed. Any who were expecting the resurrection to bring history suddenly and visibly to a halt were disappointed.

The early church, however, saw almost at once that such disappointment was inappropriate. It took the genius of Paul to unpack the whole story, but he only articulated what Christians before him seem to have grasped. Instead of the resurrection being a single, large-scale, last-minute event, it was to be seen as taking place in two stages. Jesus, having taken the role of Israel on to himself as an individual, had gone out ahead of his people, pioneering the way for them. There would still be a general resurrection, but it would come later. There would be a time-lag (see 1 Corinthians 15.20–28). And the time-lag had a purpose. It was there so that his people could go into all the world and proclaim, like messengers announcing the enthronement of a new emperor, that Jesus of Nazareth was now exalted as Lord of the whole creation. The mission of the church is the necessary link between the two resurrections, Jesus' and that of his people.

Some will no doubt see the idea of such a mission as inescapably triumphalist. Who does the church think it is, to make such announcements or proclamations? Has not a great deal of damage been done by heavy-handed religious people thundering out their own version of God's message? Well, yes, of course. But we need to pause before tarring all Christian mission with the brush of religious fanaticism. What was it, after all, that was vindicated by Easter?

It was *Jesus* who was vindicated on Easter morning. The disciples had embraced the idea of a pushy and triumphalistic mission that would leave Jesus sitting smugly on a throne in Jerusalem and themselves standing around, exceedingly pleased with themselves for having backed the right horse while still an outsider, proud now to be doing the top jobs in his 'kingdom'. Jesus' agenda had been the exact opposite of this. And it was his way of being Israel, not theirs; his way of doing God's work, not theirs, that had been vindicated on Easter morning.

And it was now his way of being Israel-for-the-world that he was passing on to his followers. '*As* the Father sent me', he said, '*so* I'm sending you.' John 20.21 summarizes the great prayer of John 17: the Father's sending of the Son to Israel now becomes the Son's sending of his Spirit-equipped people into the world.

And how had the Father sent Jesus? To confront paganism, yes. To denounce the religious, political and social idolatries that enslaved human beings, yes. But to do so, primarily, by identifying with the weak and powerless. To do so, dramatically, by being known as the friend of sinners and outcasts. To do so by apparently losing all that he had worked for, dying a cruel death as a condemned criminal. And, finally, to do so in the resurrection, which did not undo or lessen the pain or shame that had preceded it, but which vindicated that path as the one which God honoured. That, if we are to take Jesus seriously, is the pattern and model for mission that he bequeaths to his church.

What might this mean in practice? We shall spend the second half of this book working out the answer to that question.

Questions for reflection or group discussion

1 (a) Look up Philippians 2.1–5, the immediate setting for 2.5–11. In what ways does this passage set a striking agenda for the church's own life?
  (b) If Philippians 2.5–11 challenged the supreme lordship of Caesar, which supreme lordships might it challenge today?

2 If humans are made to share God's glory (see e.g. Romans 5.1–5, 8.30), how is this to be achieved, granted what we know of the human race?

3 (a) How would you summarize in a sentence the significance of the resurrection?
  (b) What difference does it make to being a Christian to realize that we live in the space between the two resurrections, Jesus' and our own?
  (c) How does believing in the cross and resurrection of Jesus affect our understanding of the meaning of the word 'God'?

Part 2

ON BEING THE CHURCH FOR THE WORLD

8

Confronting the powers

We have seen thus far that the contemporary world is full of various sorts of paganism. We have seen that on the cross, and in the resurrection, Jesus in principle defeated paganism of every sort. We must now look at the specific tasks facing the church as it confronts paganism with this gospel message, and the means that are available to the church to go about this task.

There are three classic models of how the church can respond to the challenge of paganism. The first model is simply to give up the struggle and give in to paganism. The second is to hide in a ghetto and feel artificially safe. The third is to find oneself driven to make a deeper exploration into the very nature of God himself. The first two ways, unfortunately, tend to be taken for granted within certain Christian sub-cultures. People sometimes don't even recognize other ways of responding as 'Christian' at all. This generates a good deal of puzzlement and debate.

If you can't beat them, join them

The first way of responding to paganism is the way of *assimilation*. Faced with the pagan emphasis on the goodness of creation, one part of the church will always be inclined to agree: the world is indeed a wonderful place, and we must celebrate its goodness, and stop regarding it with suspicion. Sometimes this view is taken because of the difficulty of walking the narrow road of Christian discipleship. Like the Israelites after leaving Egypt, Christians grumble: 'If only we could go back to Egypt! We had plenty to eat there,' forgetting the great act of redemption that has brought them where they are (Exodus 16.2–15).

The part of the church that thinks like this buys heavily into the theory and practice of paganism. When the culture is pointing towards money-making as the major goal in life, the church may decide to get on that bandwagon: say your prayers, contribute to the right television show, and Jesus will give you a full bank account. Plug into the right spiritual system, and your business will flourish. Wealth creation is where it's at, and the church shouldn't snipe at it, but should be glad that poverty can be alleviated. People can be rich and successful – *and* they can be Christian at the same time. This is the message, blatant and crude, of some North American televangelists. It is the message, less crude but equally clear, communicated by some 'Christian' magazines and periodicals, whose glossy advertisements proclaim the gospel of Mammon even if the product they are selling happens to be the Bible. It is also the message, dressed up in more sophisticated language, of some British and American Christians who have held advisory positions within past governments.

At the same time, the church has always been good at assimilating to the paganisms we examined in Chapter 5. We will have Jesus as our main figure of worship, but we will keep some of the other gods as well, just in case. In its mediaeval form, sneered at by enlightened modern people, this meant attributing to saints the position which pagans would assign to their ancestors. It meant all sorts of practices bordering on sympathetic magic: holy objects, holy actions, holy places, holy people, a magic holiness that would rub off on you without your knowing how. It is not sufficient to respond to such semi-paganism with a reaction that can easily be shrugged off as rationalism ('it's all mumbo-jumbo') or xenophobia ('that's the sort of thing they do in foreign countries'). If assimilation is occurring, it requires a serious theological critique, which it has not always received.

The trouble with this approach is that it is so concerned to be *like* the world that it ends up having nothing to say *to* the world. It is so concerned, to put it charitably, not to offend the noble pagan, that it refuses to call evil by its proper name and finishes by declaring that evil is simply a variant form of goodness. This has an interesting spin-off. Unless we are to say that the kingdom of God has already arrived in all its glory, we will have to give a new account of evil. How is this to be done?

When we replace the old dualisms in the church with the new monisms, 'evil' has to be relocated. The real evil, according to the proponents of pantheistic theology, is seen in the refusal of traditionalists to throw themselves into the new paganism. Everyone is in the right – Hindus, Muslims, Buddhists, New-Agers, and even some who are into witchcraft – everyone *except* old-fashioned Christians (and Jews). Dualism is the only real sin, and traditional Christianity (and orthodox Judaism) are the places where it is most clearly located.

As a result, we are witnessing the appearance of new moralities, built out of nothing except the demands of semi-Christian paganism. We have seen all this before. Who was it who said 'History repeats itself. It has to. Nobody listens'? I have written earlier about the way in which many of the churches of Nazi Germany were totally taken in by the paganism-in-Christian-clothing served up by Hitler's tame theologians. Assimilation always seems to follow a period of social or religious austerity: suddenly the brakes are off, we can freewheel downhill; suddenly everyone is rushing to affirm everything in the created order as good, and to denounce any form of restraint as anti-creation, anti-nature. (That is the message communicated powerfully by the show *Cabaret*, set in Hitler's Germany, where the casting off of all moral restraint rendered people powerless to recognize the huge evil that was looming up right in front of them.) There are many such voices audible in the church and world we inhabit today.

Assimilation, then, is always a temptation when the church faces paganism. If I am right in my analysis of paganism – that it is a parody of the Christian truth – then this should not surprise us. The truth itself is so bright and dazzling that we easily settle for alternatives that are easier to look at and live with. A monistic worldview has many attractions, but is in fact as dehumanizing for those who embrace it as for those whom its adherents attack in its name.

Back to the good old (dualistic) days

Faced with this kind of assimilationism, the natural reaction of many Christians is to draw back into a reassertion of the old Christian dualisms that characterized a former generation. If people are embracing a world-affirming paganism, some Christians will insist that the only recourse is world-denial. This option has the added attraction that it is familiar, and can therefore present itself as the 'good old way'; we know it, it's how Christianity used to be regarded by many people in our culture.

This dualistic way of being Christian, which is characteristic of conservative Christians in many different parts of the church, stands at a safe remove from everything that looks 'worldly' in the ethical sense;

from everything that looks compromised in the theological sense; and from everything that looks too 'involved' in a political or social sense. In its earlier manifestations, it was the religion of the ghetto, the lullaby of the likeminded, gently rocking sensitive Christian consciences to sleep behind firmly drawn ethical, theological and cultural lines. You knew where you were; you didn't have to think.

This dualism was reinforced from within the culture of the 1950s and 1960s by two non-Christian influences. First, there was existentialism: this world is a muddling and disorientating place, and the only thing to do is to make a decision not to be crushed by it, but to live as an authentically free human being. Many Christians in the heyday of existentialism translated the gospel into those categories, assuming a sense of disorientation (where an earlier generation would have assumed a sense of sin), and offering Jesus as the solution to the existentialist dilemma. This, of course, bought into the dualism of existentialism itself, providing an escape from the world; it was remarkably successful, however, as a starting point for evangelism. There is no reason to think, however, that it will do any good in our own day, where the more hard-nosed winners and losers in today's Western world do not sit around moaning about their inner angst.

The second reason for the popularity of old Christian dualism was the security it provided by refusing to confront the systems of the world. The world of the Enlightenment told the church not to mix religion and politics, and the church happily acquiesced, making a virtue out of this obedience by preaching about a salvation which had little relation to space and time. It is a pity nobody thought to tell St Paul about this sort of a salvation; he could have saved himself a lot of trouble in Ephesus, where his preaching against idolatry brought down the wrath of the local tradesmen's guild (Acts 19).

In our own day, resurgent dualism takes at least two forms, both of which stridently reject neo-paganism and all its works. We might distinguish them, in language borrowed from C. S. Lewis' book *The Pilgrim's Regress*, as 'dry' and 'wet' dualism respectively.

Dry dualism

The first sort of dualism I call 'dry' because it is, at its heart, very intellectual and wordy. It is a gospel for the stiff-upper-lipped. In some parts of popular evangelicalism, it presents itself as an ultra-sound restatement of old truths, and claims to possess the only true gospel. This gospel, it turns out, is that which characterized a certain kind of evangelical in (among other periods) the 1950s. The gospel and politics inhabit totally different worlds. The same is true for the gospel and the emotions, the gospel and physicality. Sexuality is deeply suspect. The sacraments are given a wide berth where possible, and handled with great caution where not. Preaching the gospel is telling people how to go to heaven when they die, and anything else is a watering down of that timeless message. It would be perfectly possible to believe this 'gospel' and go off to work every day for years without noticing that one was building the Tower of Babel.

There are other consequences. Worship must be severely ordered so as to exclude any 'Catholic' trappings. Counselling is basically done from the pulpit, not one to one. Anything which suggests loss of *control*, launching out into the unknown, taking risks in the spiritual sphere, is strictly off-limits. The charismatic movement is a snare and a delusion; modern miracles are figments of the imagination. The Bible is the authority, though it is very much the-Bible-as-read-within-the-tradition. If you suggest that biblical authority might reside in the Bible itself, with all its peculiarities and puzzles, consisting as it does mostly of stories not lists of rules and doctrines, you will be ruled out of order. This dualism (I have described the evangelical sort, because I have seen quite a lot of it, but I do not doubt that there are other sorts of 'dry' dualism around in the churches today) achieves its certainties at the expense of excluding large areas of God's world, and God's word.

Wet dualism

The 'wet' variety of dualism is much less cerebral, but lives in a no less divided world. Its 'wetness' consists in its romantic and even sentimental attachment to one type of 'Christian' culture, and its impressionistic treatment both of itself and of what it opposes. The (true) church consists of the children of light, and the rest of the world lies in thick darkness. Demons abound, and are in an incessant war with angels, who are supported when the children of light on earth say their prayers. Any signs of the 'New Age' are at once to be seen in terms of subversive demonic activity, which in some versions turns out to be closely aligned with anti-American or anti-Western-culture conspiracies. Christian life and ministry proceeds, not by faith seeking understanding, not by serious interaction with the created world or responsibility for it, but by angelic intervention, words of prophecy or wisdom from 'beyond', and by reading all events in terms of a global spiritual war. If the charismatic movement has sometimes been the means of rediscovering creation, the emotions, and the world of the Spirit, this type of dualism, into which some charismatic circles can easily slip, will warn Christians off creation, and the emotions, for good.

I do believe that there is such a thing as spiritual warfare. I do believe that prayer, including various types of prayer not always contained within the dualist worldview, is a vital weapon within this warfare. But a sort of popular dualism is, like the paganism it abhors, a caricature of the truth. It is essentially immature, inviting Christians to embrace an over-simplified world, all black and white with no shades of grey. This cannot be the way to mount a serious Christian response to neo-paganism.

These two forms of dualism, the dry and the wet, correspond very broadly to two of the dualistic movements in Jesus' and Paul's day. The Pharisees, first, had a system all worked out, in which sound loyalty to what they took to be the ancestral traditions was paramount. The Bible was read through a grid of expectations and aspirations, arising more from recent debates than from the text itself. This group saw their own position as the plain unvarnished truth, and any who demurred were simply beyond the pale. Though some Pharisees embraced political activism and even revolution in Jesus' and Paul's day, others, such as Hillel (an older contemporary of Jesus) and Gamaliel (the teacher of the young Saul of Tarsus) preached a doctrine in which the private sphere of piety was all-important. Meddling with politics took time from the study of Torah, and spoilt the pure vision of Pharisaic community. Seen from outside, the fierce debates about the details of purity look suspiciously like a displacement activity, reflecting a sense of impotence and powerlessness in the contemporary political milieu.

The Pharisees' 'dry' dualism was balanced by the 'wet' form on offer in the apocalyptic movements of the same period. The authors of works like *1 Enoch* or *4 Ezra* peopled the universe with angels and demons, diminishing the power and responsibility of humans by increasing the power of superhuman beings. Dualisms of this kind usually reflected an ethnic base, coloured in with religious language: 'we' are the children of light, 'they' (in the first century, the Romans; in the twentieth, non-Westerners) are the children of darkness. What is more, such attitudes support and sustain a military agenda. Once you have made your opponents into demons, it is not difficult to see your way to eliminating them.

'Wet' and 'dry' dualisms fail to take seriously the biblical answer to paganism. They sometimes try to focus on the cross, as I myself have done. They less frequently allow the resurrection to play its full part in their thinking. That is the task we must now attempt.

The third way: resurrection and a new vision of God

One of the exciting things about the new crisis facing Western culture, and the church within it, is that we are suddenly back on the map of the early church. Debates and issues that were run-of-the-mill in the first few centuries of the church's life, and which have been regarded as irrelevant by earlier generations, are suddenly coming to life again. The early church, like us, was faced with serious paganism within a culture that had never had the benefit of an earlier phase of Christian teaching. There is much that we can learn from those early days.

The early church inherited the Jewish tradition, which at its best understood that Israel had been called to be the light of the nations, the means by which the creator God would challenge and overcome the grip which the pagan gods had over the world. Jesus' announcement of the kingdom meant that the old gods were having notice served on them; Paul's announcement of Jesus as Lord of the world was a direct challenge to the principalities and powers that had carved up the world between them. No suggestion of assimilation can be found in these agendas; but, equally, no suggestion of dualism. The resurrection, for Paul, is the beginning of the renewal (not the abolition) of all creation, the dawning of the real New Age. 'Everything belongs to you,' he wrote to the Corinthians, 'whether it's Paul or Apollos or Cephas, whether it's the world or life or death, whether it's the present or the future – everything belongs to you! And you belong to the Messiah; and the Messiah belongs to God' (1 Corinthians 3.22–23). No dualism there!

The leading theologians of the first Christian centuries, whom we sometimes call the early church fathers, implemented that agenda. Believing that they were doing so with the guidance of the Spirit of Jesus, they totally rejected assimilation. They refused to turn Christianity into a variant form of paganism. Equally, they rejected dualism, especially of the 'gnostic' sort. Offered a religion that meant escaping from the good created order into a purely 'spiritual' sphere, they emphatically declined. In response to paganism's multiplicity of gods and goddesses, they developed and articulated the belief that the God of Abraham, Isaac and Jacob, the God who had revealed himself in Jesus of Nazareth and by the Spirit, was indeed the One God who stood over against the pagan gods. At the same time, they found that this God was best spoken of in language which reflected an irreducible threeness as well as a basic oneness. They worked out, in short, what we call the doctrine of the Trinity. They did not regard this doctrine as a piece of abstract, take-it-or-leave-it speculation. As far as they were concerned, it was the truth that made the world go round.

We shall return to the Trinity in more detail at the end of this book. For the moment we must ask: where does this new vision of God come from, and what are its implications? In the light of the previous two chapters, it should be clear that the new vision of God stems from the cross and resurrection of Jesus, and from the early church's belief that the God who had revealed himself in this way had, further, given his own Spirit to live within and empower his people. This is summed up in John's remarkable vision on the island of Patmos:

> I was in the spirit on the Lord's Day, and I heard behind me a loud voice like a trumpet . . .
>
> So I turned to see the voice that was speaking with me. As I turned, I saw seven golden lampstands, and in the middle of the lampstands 'one like a son of man', wearing a full-length robe and with a golden belt across his chest. His head and his hair were white, white like wool, white like snow. His eyes were like a flame of fire, his feet were like exquisite brass, refined in a furnace, and his voice was like the sound of many waters. He was holding seven stars in his right hand, and a sharp two-edged sword was coming out of his mouth. The sight of him was like the sun when it shines with full power. When I saw him, I fell at his feet as though I was dead.

He touched me with his right hand. 'Don't be afraid,' he said. 'I am the first and the last and the living one. I was dead, and look! I am alive for ever and ever. I have the keys of death and Hades.'   (Revelation 1.10, 12–18)

John's vision brings together the elements of the new view of God, not as abstract theory but as a summons to worship, to faith, and to obedience. Indeed, to conceive of a view of God which was *not* such a summons would be to admit defeat; if it is really God that is being thought of, the appropriate reaction can never be abstract speculation, but worship and adoration.

The vision shows just how dramatically the Jewish vision of God has been rethought. John is still emphatically monotheistic; there is no hint of assimilation to pagan ideas (the language of the vision is drawn from the Old Testament) or of world-denying dualism. But the vision of the One God has a new richness. The central figure is the one who died and is now alive for evermore, the one who has thereby defeated the last great enemy opposing the human race. The events of Calvary and Easter have put Jesus forever at the centre of the Christian view of God. But they have not displaced the central Jewish affirmation of the transcendent creator God himself. On the contrary, Jesus himself is described in imagery drawn straight from one of the central Old Testament visions of God himself (Daniel 7.9), while at the same time being also the Son of Man, the representative of God's people (Daniel 7.13). In Jesus, God and his people are united. This message is triumphantly restated in Revelation 21.

But precisely because Jesus remains Jesus, the human one, and is not as it were absorbed into a kind of omnipresent but undifferentiated divinity, it is vital that we speak also of the Spirit of God, or the Spirit of Jesus, as being sent into all the world to enable humans to be his people, to worship him and work for him in the world. In the book of Revelation as a whole, where Jesus is constantly exalted alongside the transcendent God, the role of the Spirit comes out clearly: the Spirit is the one who enables the church to be the church (2.7, 11, 17, 29, etc.; 19.10, 22.17).

This total vision is true to the entire witness of the New Testament. Although we do not find there the kind of abstract formulation of Trinitarian theology that we find in subsequent centuries, we uncover its deepest root: the conviction that in speaking of the creator God one must speak also of Jesus, and that in speaking of how this God remains active within his world in the present, one must speak of the Spirit of God, the Spirit of Jesus, making the living God present and making the love of God powerfully known.

And it is in Trinitarian theology, not as abstract speculation but as the heart of Christian worship, that the fullest and richest answer to paganism is to be found. When the early fathers hammered out this doctrine, they were articulating their belief in a God who was somehow *both* the transcendent creator, other than his world but still sustaining and caring for it, *and* the one who breathed his own life into and within the world, and was longing to fill it with his glory as the waters cover the sea. This reflects the first differentiation that, as we saw earlier, the Christian must embrace: God and the world are not the same thing, but God and the world are not to be split apart. The fathers were saying, further, that this God, who was both beyond and within the world, had acted personally within his world, to take the evil of the world into his own hands, so that the other great differentiation, that between good and evil, can be dealt with. All other philosophies or worldviews belittle the problem of evil by reducing it either in scale (it isn't so very bad after all) or in scope (it exists somewhere else, not here). The doctrine of the Trinity says, and says clearly: evil is exceedingly serious, and has infected the whole of the created order, supremely the human race; but the creator has himself taken its full force on to himself and so dealt with it. As a result, there is a new vision of the world, focused clearly on Jesus and his victory over the power that held humans in ultimate captivity: 'I died, and behold I am alive for evermore, and I have the keys of death and Hades.' And behind that, again, there is a new vision of God.

This Trinitarian worldview puts Jesus and his victory in the centre, and reshapes our view of the cosmos around that point. Nothing short of this can offer the world an integrated view of reality, which takes seriously the differentiations between God and the world, and between good and evil, without collapsing them either into spurious dualisms or into spurious assimilations. That was why the early church fathers embraced it.

There is every reason for hope as we grasp the truth of the Trinity. This is the doctrine which took on the world. Paganism offers you pleasure, but Jesus offers you joy. Dualism recommends renunciation, but Jesus promises resurrection. No wonder the early Christians changed the world. Their alternative to assimilating, or to withdrawing, was to grasp, articulate and live out the full Trinitarian worldview. This could only be done by people who were themselves grasped by the love of the God they spoke about, and who responded to that love in glad faith and obedience. They no doubt suffered from ambiguity, folly, puzzlement and misjudgment just as much as we do. But they changed the world. Their witness to this God stands firm. Our task is to discover how we may follow in their footsteps.

Questions for reflection or group discussion

1 (a) Does the worship you habitually attend reflect a fully Trinitarian sense of who God is? If not, does it tend more towards assimilating to paganism or towards a world-rejecting dualism?

 (b) How does the celebration of the resurrection change the way we look at God and the world?

2 (a) Why are people attracted towards assimilation, or towards dualism?

 (b) What problems does the Christian community meet in trying to work with Christians from backgrounds that have different traditions and emphases?

 (c) How can we escape from less-than-Trinitarian modes of worship and Christian living?

9

Equipment for the task (1)

The puzzle of the puzzles

Imagine the following scenario. You wake up one morning to find a package on your doorstep. You open it, and discover that it contains a jigsaw. The family gathers round, and begins to put it together. Over the next few days, working at it whenever you have time, you get it into what seems to be a good shape. Many of the bits quite obviously go together, and a picture is emerging. There are other bits you're not quite sure about, but they more or less fit. The picture as a whole is striking and pleasing, and the family is delighted and wants to display it somewhere.

Then, to your surprise, you discover in conversation that some friends up the street have also received a jigsaw through the post. Theirs is quite different. They, too, have had fun putting it together, have become excited at the picture that they are getting, and just a little perplexed that some of the pieces don't quite fit. Eventually, the families get together and compare jigsaws. There's a certain amount of submerged jealousy ('Ours hasn't got a border like that!' 'Theirs has that lovely bright colour in the corner!') and a certain amount of not-so-submerged pride ('*We* managed to get ours done in four days flat!' 'Ours is so much more *attractive*!'). Then one of the children notices that one of the bits their family couldn't quite figure out looks as though it might belong with one of the difficult bits in the neighbours' jigsaw.

Consternation follows:

'You mean ours is *incomplete*?'

'You're not suggesting we try and put them together?'

'That would mean taking our lovely picture to pieces, and we might never get it back together again!'

'Anyway, the two pictures are quite different! We'd get an awful hotch-potch if we even put them in the same room, let alone tried to fit them on to each other.'

At that moment, the doorbell goes, and the youngest child runs off to answer it. A moment later, she comes back to announce, with an air of triumph at being the first with the news:

'It's the lady from next door. She says can we go round some time and help her with a strange jigsaw she's had through the post . . .'

The awful truth dawns on the assembled company. Lots of jigsaws have been arriving up and down the street, *and it looks as though they are all meant to fit together.*

Enough of this parable; I hope it will make its point. I want, in this and the following chapter, to look at the surprising things that have been arriving on the doorsteps of the church over the past few years, and to suggest that they all belong together. Our God has been renewing his church in a variety of ways. One group has received a vibrant and exciting jigsaw; another, one of majestic proportions; another, one which is almost impossible to tackle; and so on. Each group is, naturally, tempted to believe that their jigsaw is the 'real' or 'true' one, and that the others are secondary deviations or distractions from it. Some are even tempted to sneer at the rest, and to deny that they have anything to offer at all. But it is my belief that the widely differing renewal movements of recent years are meant, in the last analysis, to fit together. They belong within the overall task that God has for his church in our generation. If we are to combat paganism with the gospel of Jesus, as I suggested in the previous chapter, we need all the renewal we can get. It is when we see this basic task clearly that the different bits of the larger puzzle start to drop into place.

What are the different parts of the larger puzzle? I suggest that there are at least eight, which we will look at one by one.

O worship the King

The first renewal is the renewal of *worship and spirituality.* All around the world there have been new stirrings, new life breathed into old structures, new ways of worship arising to replace outworn or sterile ones. Unlike some previous renewals in worship (for instance, that connected with the Methodist movement in the eighteenth century) this renewal is not the property of one particular movement, though there are many groups that, having had their own revival of worship, remain firmly wedded to that one style and are somewhat suspicious of the others. We must, then, look at the different areas of this renewal.

Sacramental worship

Over recent generations, a great sea-change has taken place in the worshipping habits of millions of Christians, many of them in the Anglican church but many elsewhere too. The staple diet of Anglican worship used to be Matins and Evensong, with occasional services of Holy Communion. Sometimes this was a matter of deliberate policy; many Anglicans at the Protestant end of the spectrum, deeply suspicious of Catholic sacramentalism, seemed to take delight in downplaying the role and value of the Communion service.

But a good deal of this has now changed – and, it must be said, for the better. The Bible is full of symbolism and language which comes into clear focus in the Communion, or Eucharist (the latter word, deeply suspect in some quarters, simply means 'thanksgiving'). The children of Israel in the wilderness are fed with manna from on high. Jesus, echoing this incident, tells his contemporaries that he is the true bread from heaven, and that the way to life is to feed on him. Of course this language goes far beyond the sacramental 'feeding' which takes place in the context of one church service. But to deny its plain meaning, and to play down Jesus' clear command to 'do this in remembrance of me', as has been done in some quarters, is to cut off one's nose to spite one's face.

It is a sign of real health and renewal that mainline Anglicanism has rejoined mainstream Christianity, from Calvin and the Plymouth Brethren at one extreme to the Roman Catholic and Orthodox churches at the other, in restoring the Eucharist to the central place that it obviously had in Jesus' intention and in the practice of the early church.

Liturgy

Along with this renewal, not surprisingly, has gone a renewal in liturgy. New services have been written, drawing on the best scholarship available in the attempt to reproduce in a worthy modern form the richness of older traditions, both those of traditional Anglicanism and those of other parts of the church. At their best, these liturgies have been enormously liberating. Ask any vicar whose parish includes a couple of large, mostly unchurched, housing estates whether it is easier to welcome people into a Prayer Book Matins-and-Evensong setting, or into a newly written, lively service in which all the family can join with understanding and enthusiasm. The question will answer itself.

In addition, many Christians from non-liturgical backgrounds have been discovering liturgy itself for the first time, and have been surprised and delighted by it. Some of these people come from traditional free church backgrounds, have realized that the absence of an 'official' liturgy does not prevent an 'unofficial' one from operating, and are glad to discover that it can be done in a richer and fuller way. Liturgy, properly undertaken, enables the worshipper to relax, and to focus the mind and heart, in a way rendered almost impossible if one is being jolted and tugged this way and that at the whim of those calling the chorus-numbers or 'leading worship' while apparently performing like a wannabe rock star. Liturgy, then, has made a come-back, and a real renewal of it continues to take place.

Informal worship

At the same time, there has been a parallel renewal at the level of informal worship. Many people whose experience of God (or, perhaps, simply of religion) has been in the context of dry and lifeless liturgical worship have been delighted to discover the joy of free and spontaneous worship, with a wide variety of musical styles. The House Church movement, and festivals like Spring Harvest and Greenbelt, have been among the centres of this, but it has also caught on in Anglican and other churches where the charismatic movement has taken hold. In other circles, too, including the Roman Catholic church, new musical and dramatic features have been introduced into worship. I see the movement towards a discovery of informality as complementary to the rediscovery of liturgy. Most people need *both* serious liturgy *and* informal worship at some stages at least of their spiritual pilgrimage. What we have been witnessing in both revivals, therefore, is the opening up of a range of new possibilities within the church, reviving in multiple ways the worshipping life of the whole people of God.

Spirituality

In addition to the organized worship of the church, there has been a renewal of spirituality itself. Books on prayer have become best-sellers, as people realize the poverty of many traditional patterns of private worship and devotion and search for fresh ways forward. Many Christians have realized, with a sense of liberation, that the way in which one finds it easiest to pray has a good deal to do with one's temperament. Difficulties in prayer may well result from the heavy-handed imposition of a pattern or style of prayer on someone temperamentally unsuited to it; laziness, spiritual inability, or dryness may all play a part as well, but before people start feeling guilty about that kind of thing they should enquire as to whether the sort of prayer they are attempting is the sort for which they are more naturally suited. There is every reason to suppose, in addition, that patterns of prayer can healthily develop and change with growth in the personality or different circumstances. A good deal of guilt is avoided when Christians realize this, and stop worrying about changing the habits they were taught in Sunday school.

As a result of all this, we have seen traditional boundaries breached. Evangelicals have been embracing the discipline of spiritual direction and of contemplative prayer, while Roman Catholics have discovered the 'open prayer' of the traditional evangelical prayer meeting. Other new movements in spirituality, too, are currently enriching the life of contemporary Christians. Thousands of people (for instance) have been to the ecumenical renewal centre at Taizé in France, and have come back with a new sense of awe and reverence in worship. They have been captivated by the quiet yet exceedingly powerful chants that bind together worshippers from very different backgrounds, and that seem to feed the spiritual hunger that has characterized a world starved by materialism. Thousands more have come to love the music, and the style, of Taizé worship, in transplanted settings around the world. The 'worship songs' of the 1990s and the early years of the twenty-first century have clearly impacted a generation that knew nothing of traditional church music. Though in many cases we may legitimately wonder whether these songs will have staying power, they have enabled many, particularly young people, to worship in an idiom suited to their own culture.

Worship: prospects and problems

What we have described so far in this section must be seen as a total renewal of worship. In sacrament, in liturgy, in informality and in spirituality Christians of all sorts have been discovering, as though almost by accident, the truth to which Peter Shaffer gave voice in his play *Equus*: 'Without worship you shrink. It's as simple as that.' We were once a generation of shrunken humanity, people who had forgotten how to worship. Now that we have rediscovered worship, the church, and the people within it, can begin to grow again.

There are of course problems with this. There are puzzled clashes between those who are suddenly discovering the joy of liturgy and others who are suddenly discovering the joy of informal worship. Some still nurture deep anxieties and fears about the sacraments, fearful of anything which cannot at once be reduced to safe words and thus kept under strict control. Such fears may well prove hard to allay, not least in a society where suspicion and snide put-downs are the norm. Here we must realize that the resistances we develop have to do as much with culture as theology. We live in a society with a rich mix of cultures, and it is vital to be able to discern genuine worship when contained in a cultural package with which one is unfamiliar and which may at first appear strange or threatening. What is required, in addition to the renewal of worship, is a renewal of the old-fashioned Christian virtue of *love*. When Paul wrote about this in the first century (for instance in 1 Corinthians 12—14), it had little to do with emotional feelings towards other people. It had everything to do with the glad acceptance, across traditional cultural and racial barriers, of other people who also confessed Jesus as Lord. If the church can recapture something of that spirit, then the renewal of worship will make its full contribution to our common life. In a multicultural society such as ours, any worshipper who does not feel uncomfortable with *some* aspect of a given service is either very open-minded or very sheltered from the reality of the modern church.

Part of the problem stems from seeing worship and spirituality in a box all by themselves. Worship cannot be isolated from the totality of Christian living. This jigsaw belongs with all the others. One feature of worship is that the worshippers become like that which they are worshipping; and one feature of the worship of the God revealed in Jesus and by the Holy Spirit is that worshippers of this God come to share in his concern for his whole world. Liturgy and prayer belong with the other renewal movements that God has been giving to his church, not least the movement towards a new sense of social responsibility. Worship therefore needs to be complemented by movements towards unity and towards working for God in the world. These two movements, happily, have also been under way for some time, and we must look at each in turn.

One big happy family?

Jesus prayed that his church might be one: he envisaged 'one flock, one shepherd' (John 10.16). Those who have claimed to take Jesus and his words most seriously in the past few hundred years have often, ironically, been those who have torn the church apart. They have set up rival groups and anathematized. They have broken away, broken fellowship, broken hearts and lives in the process, convinced that the unity of the church was a secondary issue and that some aspect of abstract truth was far more important. Often, those from whom they have broken away have been just as arrogant. They have assumed that, because they held positions of responsibility or authority within the church, they were automatically and inalienably in the right. The claim on both sides to possess the truth has been mixed disastrously with the reality that what both sides possessed was arrogance. If we had had genuine humility over these past few hundred years, we might well have had fewer cracks in the fabric of the new temple (1 Corinthians 3.16–17).

But in the past few years we have seen a sudden upsurge in the desire of Christians for *unity*. A generation ago, Christians from different backgrounds hardly thought of one another as Christians at all, let alone tried to engage in any conversation or dialogue. Now, churches of almost all kinds are involved, in at least some way or other, in common thought, prayer and action. In part this is no doubt due to nontheological factors in the modern world. The ease of communication, the coming together of people from differing backgrounds through travel, trade, tourism and so on – all have contributed. But I believe it is also a genuine movement, a genuine renewal, from the Spirit of God himself. So often the cracks in the church have followed the fault lines in societies: the divisions of language, race, class and so on. Sometimes (although not always) theological arguments have been manifest smokescreens for these non-theological factors. If these divisions are now being overcome, and Christians are welcoming one another with love and, in some quarters at least, with a remarkable absence of mutual suspicion, this can only be because God is enabling his people to see one another as brothers and sisters in Christ, sharing a common life, joy and hope which transcends the barriers that had kept them apart.

The unity of the church is not an optional extra. Paul, writing to the small church in Philippi to strengthen them in their witness to pagan society, says:

> then make my joy complete! Bring your thinking into line with one another.
>
> Here's how to do it. Hold on to the same love; bring your innermost lives into harmony; fix your minds on the same object. Never act out of selfish ambition or vanity; instead, regard everybody else as your superior. Look after each other's best interests, not your own . . .
>
> There must be no grumbling and disputing in anything you do. That way, nobody will be able to fault you, and you'll be pure and spotless children of God in the middle of a twisted and depraved generation . . .
>
> (Philippians 2.2–4, 14–15)

In case anyone thinks that this is idealistic advice, or just wishful thinking, it should be noted that the passage in between those two quotations holds out nothing less than the example of Jesus himself. Those who claim to belong to him cannot draw back from going the way he went. Of course there is such a thing as compromise in a bad sense, and we must beware of it. Of course there is such a thing as being sidetracked into talks about talks about talks. But the basic ecumenical vision is not one we can abandon without a far greater compromise. If the church is to take on the pagan world in our generation it must do so *with one voice*. If we do not, we are admitting before we start that the principalities and powers that ruled the world rule it still, and that the church, though an attractive idea in some ways, is powerless before them. The ecumenical renewal of the church – our growing together in love, fellowship and full union and communion – is one of the great ways in which God has been renewing his church in recent years, and when faced with our new tasks vis-à-vis the pagan world we may be able to see why. This renewal must not be allowed to run out of steam.

The challenge to the world

The church, thank God, has never lost its vision for helping those in need. There have always been those who, for the love of Christ, have gone to the rescue of the poor, the down-and-out, the untouchables of all societies. The vision of St Francis in the thirteenth century, or of Mother Teresa in more recent years, has been shared by count-less other less well known Christians who have laid aside social con-vention and expectation and gone about, as Jesus himself did, doing good and (more disturbingly) challenging the power structures that enabled evil to flourish unchecked.

This vocation of the church to *social justice*, so often squeezed to the margins of Christian existence, has received powerful new im-petus in our own day. Roman Catholic theologians in Latin America have discovered the power of the gospel of Jesus in situations of dire poverty and oppression. The church in Eastern Europe has been at the forefront of all events there, which have shaken the political frameworks within which millions of today's adults have grown up.

And, somewhere in between, groups of English-speaking Christians from backgrounds which had until recently held aloof from 'social action' as being a watering-down of the 'pure spiritual gospel' (I mean particularly Christians of an evangelical persuasion) have rediscov-ered the social dimension of that 'pure gospel'. In the United States, the Urbana mission convention and other similar gatherings have been taking the holistic dimensions of the gospel with great serious-ness. In worldwide evangelical circles, the International Fellowship of Evangelical Mission Theologians has brought together Christians with a concern for social justice from almost every corner of the globe. England has produced organizations such as Tearfund, Christian Impact Ministries and the Frontier Youth Trust who bear witness that the gospel is about more than merely saving 'souls with ears'. 'Social responsibility' is on everyone's lips, and a statement of theology that does not take it seriously is unlikely to find many adherents, except in very limited circles.

Such circles do, however, still exist. One of the reasons for this is that a good deal of the enthusiasm for translating the gospel into 'social action' has been just that – enthusiasm: the heart on fire, but the brain not necessarily totally engaged. Now, however, we have a chance to put this right. Faced with the total situation of the world, and the total task of the church in facing that world, we have the opportunity in our generation to integrate a passion for justice and peace with all other aspects of Christian living.

New dimensions in healing

In parallel to the new awareness of the plight of the poor has gone a new understanding of individual human problems. The past decades have seen a remarkable resurgence of a whole range of *healing ministries*, offering insights and experiences from an astonishingly wide range of people – monks, psychiatrists, lay workers, Orthodox and Roman Catholics as well as Protestants and evangelicals. Why has this happened?

Once again the reasons are partly sociological. We may mention three. First, our world (especially the Western world) has become a more frantic place, creating pressure and stress of which our ancestors knew nothing. At the same time, our societies have become more fragmented, with families often separated by hundreds, even thousands, of miles.

Second, we have seen a rise in the belief that human pain should by now have been eliminated by technology. Suffering is regarded as automatically and totally evil, and to be eliminated as fast as possible. If technology will not come to our rescue in a particular case, perhaps prayer will.

Third, the repaganization of the Western world has meant a swift increase in various social factors that leave deep emotional scars on many. Abortion, child abuse, the drug culture, high-pressure hard-nosed materialism, and the break-up of families: all have taken their toll.

It is my belief that God has been equipping his church to deal with this problem. Across the denominations, ministries of listening, gentleness, counselling, prayer and gifts of healing have been emerging, and many people are having their lives turned around. It is vital to emphasize the place of this renewal within the total life of the church. In Paul's celebration of the resurrection he stresses that the greatest enemies of all have been faced by Jesus and defeated:

> Death is swallowed up in victory!
> Death, where's your victory gone?
> Death, where's your sting gone?

> The 'sting' of death is sin, and the power of sin is the law. But thank God! He gives us the victory, through our Lord Jesus the Messiah. (1 Corinthians 15.54–57)

And if the greatest enemy has thus been brought low, why should we balk at the thought of lesser victories that will follow? There is a strange reluctance among some Christians to admit that God can bring radical change to the inner, or the outer, life of those who believe in him. But if we believe in a God who has already defeated death itself, then we cannot discount such secondary victories, over the emotional, psychological and physical wounds that distort and deface human lives. To put it crudely, I cannot believe that when Jesus said 'greater works than these you will do, because I go to the Father' (John 14.12) what he actually meant was 'lesser works than these you will do'.

Once again, it is possible to make this kind of ministry the be-all and end-all of the Christian gospel. There are those who, fired with all the zeal of the convert, discover a new dimension to inner healing and then proceed as if all problems of all sorts could be addressed by the same means. There are those who, having witnessed a remarkable physical healing, assume that all physical ailments must be healed as quickly and easily. Equally, there are those whose real goal is a kind of universal existentialist panacea: the aim is to enable as many humans as possible to live happy and untroubled lives. Such an attitude hardly does justice to Jesus' call to take up the cross and follow him. Such mistakes are, clearly, those of the family that idolizes its own jigsaw and fails to see that there might be other complementary ones.

But there are equal and opposite mistakes. It is, for instance, foolish to pooh-pooh or marginalize the healing and counselling ministry. There are those who, with their own emotions under lock and key, are impatient of those who have nervous breakdowns or mid-life crises, or of people who suffer from stress, nervous tension, depression or less obvious emotional ailments. There are those who, aware of the possibility of being deceived in such matters, try to dismiss all suggestion of physical healing as wishful thinking, and others who suggest that all emotional problems come from unconfessed sin or lack of true faith. Such attitudes, I think, are cruel and thoughtless. Many people, including many Christians, find themselves at the pressure points of modern society, and sometimes the pressure becomes intense. To escape from the pain by pretending one has no emotions is to be a Stoic, not a Christian. To seek help where help has been provided by God is not a sign of being unwilling to stand on one's own two feet. It is a sign of humility, and an evidence of the mutual support of the body of Christ.

The counselling and healing ministries are therefore, I suggest, further renewal movements with which God has been blessing his church in the recent years. It is important to stress again that this renewal does not come in order that Christians may simply lead lives of untroubled ease. When God heals someone's body, memory, imagination, thought-life or will, it is not simply so that the person concerned may from then on be a happy, self-sufficient Christian existentialist, living for themselves alone. It is so that they may be set free from the things which have prevented them from serving Christ in his world. It is so that they may then give themselves to the renewal of God's church.

We have now looked at four key ways in which God has been equipping his church for the tasks which lie ahead. These jigsaws must be put together, and allowed to contribute to one another. Once we accept that different segments of the church have been 'renewed' in different ways, and that we need one another's renewals to flesh out our own, we will be able to face our new tasks with courage and confidence. But the puzzle is not yet complete. There are four more renewal movements to be considered.

Questions for reflection or group discussion

1 (a) Which of the renewals described above, if any, has characterized your church, or have you experienced personally?
   (b) What problems have you encountered as a result?
   (c) What new dimensions has it opened up in your (individual or corporate) life?

2 (a) In what ways might you, or your church, be able to experience some of the renewals described above which have not yet affected you? What might you miss if this doesn't happen? What might you lose if it does? Need it be a case of new wine bursting old bottles, or can there be less violent ways forward?

10

Equipment for the task (2)

We have now looked at four ways in which God has been renewing his church in recent years, to meet the challenges that lie ahead. I now want to suggest four more. We begin in what to some will be an unlikely place.

Be adult in your thinking

The word 'adult' has come to have a seedy meaning. If we pass a shop with the words 'Adult Books' above it, we know what to expect: material of such low grade that no self-respecting child would want anything to do with it. That is why, looking back to the pagan society of the first century, we find St Paul warning the Christians in ultra-pagan Corinth to be 'youngsters when it comes to evil' (1 Corinthians 14.20). If being grown-up means getting into the sordid world of 'adult' occupations, better stay a child. But Paul is not recommending human immaturity. On the contrary, he is warning against it. The so-called 'adult' world of pornography, and many other evils by which humans exploit one another, offer a spurious human maturity. The real sort, Paul insists, involves growing up in a much more rigorous, but much more rewarding way: be adult, he says, in your *minds* (1 Corinthians 14.20).

At once some contemporary Christians go hot and cold all over. The one thing we don't want is to be made to *think*. Experts, egg-heads, educationalists – we've had enough of them. I have a feeling that this is a peculiarly British disease; I do not observe it in the same way in North America, say, or Germany. In France, too, the word 'intellectual' is still (I understand) a praise-word. In England it is usually a term of veiled, or not so veiled, abuse.

God has, nevertheless, been renewing the *thinking* of his people. When I returned from teaching in North America to England, I was surprised and delighted to discover that the number of young people who wished to read theology at a university had gone up substantially over the previous years. That trend may be significant. There is, among many young people today, a hunger for teaching about God, about the meaning of life. Wherever people take the trouble to put on adult education days or weeks, or summer schools, about the Christian faith, lay people turn up, often at considerable personal cost and sacrifice. They listen carefully, take notes, and ask searching and intelligent questions. Often, I think, the clergy underestimate the genuine and widespread desire to *learn*. There are lots of people in and out of the church with first-class minds (note, I do not say 'with first-class educations'), who know a good argument when they hear one, and want to hear more, especially when they concern God.

And God has been equipping the church to address this felt need, to think through the Christian faith and its relevance. The task of shepherding the flock of Christ clearly involves a commitment to lead the thinking and reflecting of God's people, and we have seen an encouraging increase in the number of people willing to engage in this task. There are far more people engaged in theological research now than there were many years ago, and a good deal of them are people with a deep and strong personal Christian faith. Organizations which were set up to help people study the Christian faith and its implications a generation ago have grown far beyond their founders' expectations. Books, magazines, serious studies of serious theological topics, are now readily available. There is no excuse now for being an uneducated Christian. The materials are all to hand.

Here too, of course, there are pitfalls. The kingdom of God is not necessarily substantially advanced just because another bright young Christian graduate completes her PhD thesis, nor because some enterprising young lecturer publishes a learned article setting out his new interpretation of 2 Timothy 4.3. The public at large, not least in the churches, remains puzzled by the hair-splitting of scholars, who seem often to pursue their own agendas, their own private tidyings-up of texts or historical periods. And if the scholar ventures out of his or her own territory, the response is likely to be the sneering suggestion that one should stick to one's subject. All it takes is for one biblical scholar to say something silly (and scholarship is no more of a guard against silliness than any other profession) and some Christians write off all biblical scholarship as a waste of time, not realizing that they become thereby dependent on the biblical scholarship of two generations ago, filtered through the memory of their regular preacher.

But if the church is to face the tasks which lie ahead in the next generation it must not retreat *either* into the private intellectual games of detached scholarship (which are themselves often a defence mechanism against the slings and arrows of a critical world) *or* into the anti-intellectual passivity that so easily grips Christian people today. Put the mind into neutral, and what you will get is not Christianity, but some form either of dualism or, more likely, of paganism. The challenge to think clearly is part of the challenge to be Christian. The challenge to think Christianly is part of the calling to the church to take on the world with a gospel which makes sense; which makes biblical sense; which makes sense of things for which the world of paganism has no answer. God has been renewing his church in its thinking, so that it can address the world the more clearly.

New light from the Word

'God has yet more light to break out of his holy word.' This celebrated remark, variously attributed to a number of godly folk from previous generations, has shown fresh signs of coming true in our own day. The Bible has long been at the centre of the worshipping and reflecting life of the church, and one aspect of the renewal of the church's thinking and learning has been a willingness on almost all sides to take the Bible seriously and wrestle with its message. We have seen a real renewal in *biblical study* within the past few generations.

This has taken a variety of forms. To begin with, there have been more biblical commentaries available, at all levels from the most thorough and academic to the most popular and user-friendly, than at any time before. Behind this, there has been an explosion of knowledge in the fields of enquiry that service the study of the Bible. Lexicons, concordances, new translations, books exploring every aspect of biblical culture, theology, genres and so on abound. At the same time, there has been in some quarters a revival of interest in expository preaching. The art of so opening a passage of scripture that members of a congregation feel themselves addressed by it has never been entirely lost, and today more preachers are rediscovering the excitement of puzzling over a text until it becomes part of them, and then sharing their discoveries with others. This is a wonderful movement, and cannot but improve the health of the church.

Again, creative new ways of studying the Bible have been opened up. Many who have been bored by Bible studies where the leader asked trivial questions or drew trivial insights out of a passage have had their interest rekindled by exploring different possibilities. Poetic texts have been studied and enjoyed as poetry. Prayerful texts have been turned into actual prayer. Dramatic texts have been acted out: many have found the gospels coming alive in new ways in the hands of a skilled solo actor, and I shall not forget the impact of Galatians 'performed' by an actor/scholar during a conference several years ago. There are more possibilities in this area waiting to be discovered and appropriated.

Furthermore, branches of Christianity that were not traditionally known for their enthusiastic study of the Bible have in some cases begun to read it with new eyes. The use made of scripture by liberation theologians has caused many eyebrows to be raised in conservative circles. It is, however, beyond question that such use, for all its ambiguities, has brought to light aspects of the many-faceted message of the Bible which had long been forgotten. Equally, Roman Catholic theologians have felt a new freedom to explore scripture and apply what they have found to the life of the church and world, often with startling results.

At the same time, such readings have exposed the one-sidedness of many ways of reading the Bible in other parts of the church, in which all too often the prejudices of the Enlightenment have been first read into the text and then triumphantly proclaimed as though the text itself supported them. Equally, in more conservative groupings, a particular theological stance, long assumed to be 'biblical' and therefore valid, can become so powerful that it will actually muzzle anything in the Bible that threatens it. A good example of this is the emasculation, in many conservative circles, of Paul's famous letter to the Romans. I have often witnessed Christians from this background emphasizing the first eight chapters and ignoring the last eight, though this in fact grossly distorts the entire letter. There are still difficult and often contentious debates about what precisely we might, or should, mean by 'the authority of scripture', and a good deal of work needs to be done on this issue (I have tried to sketch out the groundwork for this in my book *Scripture and the Authority of God*). But the text remains there for all to see, and it still possesses an astonishing capacity to challenge fixed assumptions and propose new perspectives.

My main contention in this section is, I think, beyond question. God has been restoring to his church a sense of wonder and excitement, a fascination with and love for the Bible. And this is bound to continue to contribute to the renewal of the church as a whole for the new tasks which God is setting before us.

The whole people of God

A seventh area in which God has been renewing his church is that of *lay ministry*. Not so long ago, the average church, whether Roman Catholic, Anglican, Methodist or whatever, was largely a 'one-man-band' (and it was, of course, emphatically a 'one-*man*-band'). The few lay people who rallied round to help with odd jobs, whether counting the collection or repairing the tiles on the roof, were welcomed, but there was not much sense that they were sharing in the work of ministry itself. Shepherding the flock was a specialized task, and a jealously guarded one at that.

Now all that has changed. 'Every-member ministry' is here to stay, at least in theory. Most clergy believe that the laity have important gifts that must be utilized if the church's ministry is to be complete; some actually put this belief into practice. This is often hard both for the clergy, who have to delegate things they might traditionally have done themselves, and for the laity, who find themselves called to abandon a sleepy passivity and take on responsibilities for things within the church. But in many areas a whole new attitude to worship, evangelism, the caring ministries, and so on, has been the result. We have come to see that for professional shepherds to keep the care of the flock to themselves is for the flock to be under-nourished, badly cared for and lacking in a sense of direction. The tasks need to be spread more widely, for the good of the whole community.

Once more, there are sociological reasons for this new move, as well as theological ones. The general mood of anti-authoritarianism in Western society is partly responsible for the shift, and this can be seen when those who are eager to embrace lay ministry (and to argue for it from scripture) are slow to grasp those parts of the Bible which speak of different ministries, commanding respect and obedience, entrusted to certain office-bearers within the church. Equally, there are those whose arguments against lay involvement in the church are part of a wider social agenda, of keeping at bay any attacks on traditional authority structures. The only cure for such a Canute-like position may be to deal with the deeply ingrained fears that prevent such a person from opening up to receive what God is giving to his church today.

The new moves towards the involvement of every member of the church in some kind of ministry are too vital and important to be held at bay by quibbles. Nor should it be thought that 'lay ministry' means, or can be confined to, non-ordained people presiding at worship services, or administering the Communion chalice. It is not a matter of 'lay ministry' in church so much as out in the world. The church must recognize, encourage and enable its members to act, in the world, not as private individuals but as part of the whole body of Christ. We desperately need Christians to be active *as* Christians in the workplace; not simply to organize shop-floor Bible studies or in-house evangelistic events, but to do their work from a Christian perspective and on a thought-out Christian basis. We particularly need Christians in the media – in television, radio, the video industry, and journalism, all of which reach more people by far than ever come to church or read a 'serious' book. We need more top-quality Christian artists, playwrights, and composers. We need more Christian businessmen and women, who will not only conduct their businesses with the Christian ethic in mind but will also reflect Christianly and creatively on where commerce is going in the modern world. We need Christian bus drivers, Christian teachers, Christian secretaries, Christian builders, Christian lawyers, Christian nurses, Christian computer-programmers, who will know what they are doing and why.

And the church, as it finds that such people belong to its number, is to teach, train and enable all of them to minister where they are, not simply in one-to-one personal ministry, vital though that is, but in making a serious Christian contribution to the direction of their profession, their business, or their trade. For too long the church has allowed its members to go to work with a high-grade professional qualification in one pocket and a Sunday-school faith in the other. The gospel is easily big enough, and tough enough, for the needs of lay people working for Christ in the world. If we grasp the fact that

God has been encouraging a renewal in lay ministry, and put it in the context of all the other renewals that are in progress, we have the makings of a new movement whose potential is incalculable.

The rushing mighty wind

Perhaps the greatest of the renewal movements that God has sent his church in the past few years is the one that is often given the name '*renewal*' itself. For many decades now, often unexpectedly and usually inconveniently, Christians from a wide variety of backgrounds have experienced a great inner and corporate renewal which they have attributed directly to the Holy Spirit. The charismatic movement has caught up millions of previously sleepy or stuck-in-the-mud Christians. It has brought spontaneity and joy to churches and individuals alike. It has itself been a part-agent of many of the renewals of which I have already spoken. It has produced a new liberty and delight in worship. It has engendered a new freedom in prayer. It has often resulted in an increased concern for the welfare of those around, and a new enthusiasm for fellowship across traditional denominational barriers. One of its major characteristics has been a new awareness of the healing power of God. It has frequently made people read the Bible with new eyes, and it has regularly contributed to the mobilization of lay people for the work of Christ.

It is important, of course, to recognize that the charismatic movement is not of itself the solution to all the church's ills. Cynics may well comment that it has sometimes encouraged individualism and fragmentation of churches. Often it has fostered anti-intellectualism. Sometimes it has looked suspiciously like the spirit of the age, for instance when offering 'good feelings' as though for their own sake. Sometimes it has merely offered a new religious experience for bored evangelical existentialists. It has sometimes led people into a new radical dualism: anything 'charismatic' is of God, anything else is of the devil. It has the capacity to engender a new authoritarianism: having liberated people, it has put them into new little boxes. It has bred its own stultifying para-liturgies, forms of words (whether of men or of angels) which have ceased to function as words and have become merely mantras. And tragically, aping the worst of modern advertisements, it has sometimes held out easy solutions to people with deep needs and hurts, producing disappointment, anger and cynicism.

But the charismatic movement, at its best, has emphasized and enhanced the goodness of God's creation and the importance of being in touch with one's total self as a human being. It has continually reminded soporific Christians that they can and must wake up, and that the power to work for Christ in the world comes not from their own unaided efforts but from the Wind of God, the wind that blew over the waters of creation, the wind that caught up the disciples on the day of Pentecost. It has been, in countless cases, the instrument of those words of Jesus in John's gospel coming true: I came, he said, so that people may have life, and have it in all its fullness (John 10.10).

And, if the church is to attempt any of the tasks which I shall discuss in more detail in the next two chapters, the only possible way it can do so is if it believes that the Spirit of the living God is alive and well and at work, not only when we read the Bible and pray and 'evangelize', but also, and perhaps particularly, when in Jesus' name we confront the neo-paganisms of the modern world, and when in Jesus' love we groan with the groanings of those caught up in the dehumanizing effects of that neo-paganism. And if that makes 'charismatics' of all of us, so be it.

Party spirit: the hazard of renewal

As we conclude this pair of chapters dealing with the various renewals that God has been giving to his church, a word on the state of 'parties' and groups within the church. Tragically, it has often been the case that a renewal can become a special-interest group, and a special-interest group can become a party. Allegiance to the party is then deemed to constitute allegiance to the renewal that occasioned it. Within Anglicanism, this has happened, notoriously, with the 'catholic' party, giving allegiance to a renewal which happened in the nineteenth century; with the 'evangelical' party, aligning itself with historic renewals in the sixteenth and eighteenth centuries, and with some more recent movements; with the 'liberal' party, claiming to support the rise of historical consciousness through the Enlightenment, and a variety of other 'modernist' causes; and with the 'charismatic' party, coming in on the tide of the various Pentecostal movements of the last century. What are we to say about such things?

When I was asked to speak at the Greenbelt festival several years ago, I was faced with the question 'What is an evangelical?' as the title for one of my sessions. I suggested in return that I might be allowed to reshape the question. I felt it more helpful to ask the following question: what tasks is God calling the church to in our generation? And, *in the light of this*, we may ask: what resources are there within evangelicalism (or Catholicism, or liberalism, or the charismatic movement, or anywhere else) that equip us for this task? One might add: what is there within any of these traditions which is actually holding us back from addressing this task? I believe that unless we look at things this way round, we will be like Red Cross officials debating the merits of different types of stretchers while all around them lie wounded people awaiting treatment. If there was ever a time for defining parties, it is now long past, and the only purpose such a task could serve would be a negative and inward-looking one at a time when the world desperately needs a positive and outward-looking church. It is vital that, with all the renewals that the church is experiencing, we do not lapse into new parties, or variations of the old ones, but allow the church to grow together and present a united front to the world. It is time to forget evangelicalism and concentrate on the gospel; to forget Catholicism and concentrate on the church and its mission; to forget liberalism and concentrate on clear thinking; and to forget the charismatic movement and invoke the Spirit of the living God.

This is emphatically not a plea for unthinking pragmatism. Nor am I denying that the church has learnt important lessons during its history, which we forget at our peril. Nor, again, is it a way of saying that we should now sit loose to all previous doctrinal formulations. I cherish the foundation doctrines of Christianity, seeing in them a tried and trusted statement of truth and a guide for the church. But doctrine, clung to as a drowning swimmer clings to a raft, is not the essence of Christianity. What matters is to grasp, and even more to be grasped by, the God of whom all doctrines speak. My plea, therefore, is that we recognize God as sovereign over all our divisions; that we see the Bible itself as sovereign over all our traditions, including those that claim the Bible as their own; that we allow the Spirit free play in our churches, and remain open to the possibility of learning new things from unexpected quarters. This is a plea that we should put the horse before the cart. It is a plea to look outwards, and to allow the different renewal movements that we have experienced to enable the church to be the church *for the world.*

Questions for reflection or group discussion

1 (a) There is a difference between *experiencing* a renewal for oneself and *recognizing* that it has taken place, and that others have profited from it. Which of the renewals are for everybody, and which is it legitimate to recognize without necessarily sharing in?

2 (a) How can we test signs of renewal, to see whether they are really of God or merely the bright idea of an ingenious innovator?
   (b) How can we overcome suspicion and division within the church at signs of renewal?
   (c) How can we preserve the best of the past while still being open to new life?

3 In what ways (if any) has the charismatic movement in particular affected you and your church? How can Christians of all backgrounds be the channels of the power of God's Spirit in the world today?

11

New shrines for the true God (1)

We have now looked at some of the renewal movements with which God has been enriching his church in recent years. It is my contention in this book that these movements have been preparing us for the new tasks that now await us. In this and the next two chapters we will examine some of these tasks, which consist of confronting paganism with the gospel of Jesus.

Planting the flag in hostile soil

If you go to some of the sites where archaeologists have dug up Roman remains around Britain, not least in the area of Hadrian's Wall, you will discover an interesting phenomenon. The Romans, or some of them, began by a certain period to worship Jesus, and so they built and used small churches. And quite often they built their churches on top of earlier, non-Christian places of worship. If you dig down beneath the Christian stonework, you will often find an earlier shrine, perhaps to Mithras or one of the other pagan gods favoured by the Roman army in earlier times. The same is true right across the early Christian world.

Why did they do this? Wasn't it rather odd, or even offensive? What would the Mithras-worshippers think? Might it not be a bit risky, suggesting that former Mithras-worshippers could carry on worshipping in the old way with just a new name for the same god?

It seems to me that the instinct those builders were following was basically sound, and one which we need to recapture. In this chapter and the next I shall suggest that we ought to be doing substantially the same thing in our own generation, not necessarily with buildings, but in more subtle ways. For too long we have stood by and watched as paganism has won the allegiance of millions. This victory, like the earlier conversion to Christianity, has its architectural symbols: the skylines of our cities, which used to be dominated by the spires and towers which reminded citizens of a God who transcended their world, are now dominated by the tower-blocks and skyscrapers which assert that Mammon rules the world. It is time to work out, and put into practice, ways of asserting, clearly and firmly if humbly and wisely, that Jesus is Lord, and that the usurping powers of paganism are just that: usurpers.

This is substantially what Jesus did when he came to the tomb of Lazarus and confronted the powers of death with a word more powerful still. Martha came to Jesus, still in the grip of grief at her brother's death: 'Lord,' she said, 'if you had been here, my brother would not have died.' Jesus' response to her is to invite her to replace death as the centre of her attention with himself. 'I am the resurrection and the life,' he said (John 11.25). The main line of our approach to the deadly forces in our world must be the same: that we insist on worshipping Jesus in the place where other forces, other gods, at present hold sway.

The key to it all is for us to realize that paganism provides a *parody* of Christianity. It is as though Christianity is the tune which paganism sings in the wrong key, the true picture of which paganism sketches a caricature. Paganism gets its force, as does a caricature, by emphasizing one aspect of the good, God-given created order, at the expense of other aspects. Christianity, in response, must present the true picture which will enable people to see the caricature for what it is. If this means planting flags in hostile soil, so be it. It is the Christian claim that every square inch of the world, every split second of time, belongs to Jesus, by right of creation and by right of redeeming love.

At this point, though, some will be alarmed at the thought that we should disturb the paganism all around us. Surely one of the fundamental things about Christianity is living and letting live? Surely it means being nice to one's neighbours? Well, yes and no. If my neighbour is abusing his children, being nice to him may involve giving the children shelter and calling the police. If my neighbour is painting racist slogans on the walls, being nice to her may involve confronting her with the truth that all humans are made in the image of the One God. Subtler, more 'civilized' forms of paganism may not stand out so obviously, but they are there and must be dealt with appropriately. Otherwise we are not worshipping Jesus, but the Enlightenment's parody of Jesus: the Jesus who merely went about being nice to everyone, and who is rather different from the stern and puzzlingly confrontational (as well as wonderfully gentle) Jesus of the gospels.

Like Paul in Athens, then, we must take the risk of affirming the goodness of the world, and of affirming Jesus within that context. In Acts 17 he preaches a sermon, taking up the text he found on a wayside pagan altar: 'To an unknown god'. 'Well: I'm here to tell you about what it is that you are worshipping in ignorance,' he declared (Acts 17.23). Some (dualists, of course) have criticized Paul for this. But it seems to me exactly right. Paganism is a feeling after the truth. It is like a moth trying to fly to the moon: it is true that there is light to be found there, but unfortunately there is no heat, and no atmosphere to fly for most of the journey. It is a deception. Paganism is the same. It shines with borrowed light, luring unsuspecting humans towards a goal which cannot in fact be reached and which would offer no warmth if it could. *But this does not mean that there is no such thing as the sun.*

My major suggestion in this half of the book is that we should copy the early church, and Paul, in finding out where pagan gods and goddesses are being worshipped, and finding ways of worshipping Jesus on the same spot. In old pietist language, if he is not Lord of all, he is not Lord at all. What is at stake here is not just ecclesiastical policy or reshaping bits of tradition. It is the sovereignty of Jesus, the power of the Spirit, and the goodness and love of the creator God – in short, the doctrine of the Trinity and the Christian way of life which goes with it.

We must work out what it might mean in practice to take on the pagan gods and goddesses with the gospel of Jesus. There are seven areas in which I propose that new shrines are to be built. I begin, in the present chapter, with two of the most obvious ones.

Mars

The god of war is still very much in business. Of course national and international security are important, and are sometimes to be maintained by what is effectively an international police force. But the makers of war – those who research and manufacture weapons and their supporting technology – are exceedingly powerful, and, when they call the tune, governments start to sing.

Our international scene gives extensive evidence of Mars-worship, but it is noticeable that violence is on the increase at local levels also. There are many towns and cities in the Western world where in some areas it is no longer safe to walk down the street alone. Violence is glorified in films, videos, and novels, and acted out on the streets and in homes. Where we once had, in the West, a society where everybody at least gave lip-service to the principle that forgiveness was a good thing, we are now moving rapidly towards the state where it is seen as a sign of weakness. Hitting back is the norm. Mars rules, and the sacrifices that are offered at his shrine are usually human ones.

And the church dare not, must not, respond to this with the casual simplicities of dualism. Like all paganisms, Mars-worship consists of a proper motive – the obligation to protect the weak from evil – distorted and enlarged out of all proportion. We cannot simply pretend that we live in two worlds, that wars don't matter because people are going to die sooner or later anyway and what matters is the state of their souls. Nor can we settle for a cheap pacifism whose local analogue would be the disbanding of the police force and the law courts. There is such a thing as wickedness in the world; the weak must be protected from it, and those tempted to put it into practice must see that it will not pay in the end.

Rather, the church must work to find creative and non-violent ways of resolving conflict. If we are to build shrines for Jesus on territory at present occupied by Mars, it will not do to enter the discussion at the point where things have already gone too far. It is vital that the church be involved, prayerfully and then vocally, in the earliest stages of international disputes, working together with Christians in other countries to understand local feelings, to see in advance where trouble is likely to come, and to take steps to be bridge-builders and peacemakers wherever possible. The church should give itself to this task, not as a hobby, aside from its major work, but as a serious and vital part of its witness to the Prince of Peace. It should be training those of its members who have gifts for this task, providing them with the resources and support necessary to build up local, national and international networks of peacemaking. At the moment it has often been content to let the job be done by small special-interest organizations, while the rest of the church looks on from a distance, regarding such activity as somewhat suspect.

In addition, it is vital that the church seek out and care for the victims of the idolatry of others. There are whole communities, whole nations, as well as individuals and families, whose lives have been torn into shreds by wars not of their own making. If the church belongs anywhere in our world it belongs right there. It must come alongside those in pain and share their sorrow, without calculating the costs or spin-offs. The followers of the crucified Lord can do no less.

Mammon

A good deal of the support for Mars comes from the fact that the societies in which his cult flourishes are worshipping Mammon. We have already noted the way in which the skyscrapers of our cities function, as cathedral spires did before, as symbols to indicate which gods are being worshipped. Increasingly, in our society, money has taken over the all-powerful position, so that large numbers of graduates each year do not think of going to work in creative or cultural areas, but simply want to enter the business of handling other people's money, of playing number games that circle the world in a kind of giant corporate roulette. The great financial crash of 2008 caused many to question all this, but now the game is back in action once again, as fast and ruthless as before.

One indication of this is the periodical *The Economist*. In theory, it offers what its title suggests: serious discussion of economic issues. In practice, it expands the territory of economics so as to include all of human life. Its sections on art and literature, on music and theatre make the point by their very presence: economics is the science of life. This is nothing less than a total worldview. I am only half joking when I say that I would like to see a serious Christian periodical, *The Theologian*, that would do the same, making the point that theology, so far from being the irrelevance that most, not least most politicians, imagine, is in fact the real science of life. But that is another matter.

Mammon, like all idols, enslaves and dehumanizes not only those who worship him but also those who are caught in his net. Societies where Mammon is worshipped are societies where the poor are despised: they obviously haven't worshipped the god properly, unlike the rest of us who have received the rewards that he offers. Societies where Mammon is worshipped are societies where millions of people are kept in debt, and hundreds of people are kept in clover. That was the situation in the Palestine of Jesus' day, and it isn't surprising that one meaning of one of the clauses in the Lord's Prayer is 'forgive us our debts'. It will not do to reply that people simply shouldn't get into debt. That may well be the right response to our fast-credit Western society. It is emphatically not the right response to current debt in the global South, and in some areas in our modern cities. There, debt is inevitable, and those with enough and to spare continue to profit from the misfortune of others.

What can be done about Mammon? It is part of the lie put about by his worshippers, not least in the political and financial institutions in our society, that nothing can be done about him, and indeed that he must be left to himself, since only thus will society find its natural way forward. But that means, to put it bluntly, that Jesus is not Lord of the world; that on the cross he did not, after all, defeat the principalities and powers that enslave human beings. Equally, however, we should not imagine that a complex society can do without money. Mammon-worship, like other idolatries, is a distortion of a God-given resource. How then can we celebrate Jesus' lordship in territory where the devotees of Mammon are currently worshipping?

To begin with, we must follow the example of Jesus and identify with the plight of the poor. It is shocking to say it, but a phrase like that has come to be seen as such a left-wing slogan that many Christians are instantly suspicious of it. I cannot see, however, that the example of Jesus and the fact of rampant Mammon-worship in our society leave us with any choice. The church must urgently address the task of getting alongside the poor, not only in far distant parts of the globe but in our own society. Some churches are making excellent headway with this. Others need to follow suit.

This means, effectively, that we must put Mammon back in his place. Money, like fire, is a good servant but a bad master. The various New Testament injunctions to give things (including money) away, without counting the cost, may read like foolishness in our Mammon-crazed society. They are, in fact, invitations to celebrate the fact that Jesus is Lord and Mammon isn't. They are balanced, of course, by commands to provide for one's family, and so on: the early church included many who retained property and used it to the glory of God and the furtherance of the gospel, as well as many who gave all away and followed Jesus. In our modern world, too, there will be many whose vocation includes the calling to provide for their families, and to support the church in its varied work; and this can only be done through the appropriate use of money. There will also be those who are called to demonstrate the lordship of Jesus, and the dethronement of Mammon, by living without possessions, sharing the poverty of the many who are crushed by Mammon and his devotees. The church has a responsibility to support and encourage more of its members to take this route as and when they are called to do so.

In addition, the church must engage, as a matter of urgency, in an analysis of the causes of world poverty and its potential cure. I have seen it argued that if the Western world took a twenty per cent drop in its living standards for a year or two (which many of us could well sustain), the problem of world poverty could be solved, whereupon the living standards of all could return to where they were before, if not better. Such an act of repentance and trust would, of course, be unthinkable in today's world, but only because our society has bought so heavily into Mammon-worship. The churches need to be in command of such arguments, and the detailed analyses which support them, and present them with reason and vigour in the necessary quarters.

Mars and Mammon are two of the pagan deities that have enslaved millions in our own day. We must not be deceived by them. They were defeated when Jesus died on the cross; in his resurrection he is enthroned as the Lord who rules over them and the whole world. We must therefore, as Paul commanded the Colossians, seek the things that are above, worshipping Jesus above all things, and bringing our own lives, and the life of our society, into obedience to him. The false gods will scream that obedience to Jesus Christ is dehumanizing, unnatural, unworkable, destructive, undemocratic, unfair. This is mere projection. They will continue to hold out the bait of 'freedom', hiding the hook of slavery behind it. We must calmly and prayerfully resist their threats.

Questions for reflection or group discussion

1 (a) What is your initial reaction to the suggestion that we might build shrines for Jesus on ground occupied by pagan shrines? Are you excited? Cross? Anxious? Can you think why?
  (b) What reaction can the church expect if it attempts the tasks outlined here?

2 (a) Which major idols are most obviously worshipped in your area? What is your church doing about it?
  (b) Can you see how the idol of technology is worshipped, what its effects are, and how you might worship Jesus in its place?

3 (a) How can the leading churches realistically oppose the worship of Mammon, while themselves (in England at least) remaining major and wealthy property-owners?
  (b) Can you suggest more practical ground-claiming exercises in these areas, at individual, local, national, and international levels?

12

New shrines for the true God (2)

We have looked at two of the pagan gods and goddesses who have been worshipped in our society for some time. Now, beginning a further set of such deities, we must look at another extremely well-known one.

Aphrodite

The goddess Aphrodite, the goddess of erotic love, has made a big come-back in the past generation or two. She used to be worshipped openly in the ancient world, either under that name or under her Latin name, Venus. In more recent years, especially in the nineteenth century, Western culture kept her discreetly veiled. Eroticism has always existed, of course. No culture has been without it. And this is hardly surprising: when God made humans, he made them in his own image, male and female. There is something about sexual attraction in general, and in particular about the complementarity between maleness and femaleness, which resonates so powerfully in the human subconscious, which catches so many echoes of the meaning of creation itself, that it is only right that erotic love should be accorded an important place in human society and culture. That is one reason why the Song of Songs has a vital and valued place within the canon of scripture.

The problem comes when, as in our own day, this God-given aspect of being human is made the be-all and end-all of human existence. Eroticism is the pagan caricature of the God-given sexual desire. It implies that sexual activity is the cure-all, the greatest good, the one thing for which we were made. Newspapers and magazines scream this message at us; advertisement hoardings hit us in the face with it. The goddess Aphrodite offers bliss, escape, transports of delight.

The odd thing is that she repeatedly fails to deliver on those promises. With all the modern literature of the 'how-to-have-good-sex' variety, with all the freedom to talk and discuss, with all the modern therapies and counselling, I am constantly aware as a pastor that sexuality remains for many people a puzzling and paradoxical aspect of their humanness. Those who worship Aphrodite may sacrifice many things at her altar: time, money, deep or lasting relationships, unborn children, emotional maturity, secure jobs, health and even life itself. She remains inscrutable, holding out glittering promises which turn out to be mirages. And yet her worshippers come back for more.

The answer to the worship of Aphrodite cannot be to deny that she has real power. Many Christians from many traditions, seeing the shipwreck others have made in this area, and perhaps frightened of their own deep longings and emotions, have retreated into dualism. Let us push out of sight all sign that we are sexual beings, and maybe Aphrodite will go away and leave us alone. The result can be tragic. Homes where sexuality is firmly repressed may be places where secret sexual abuse flourishes. Humans who deny that they are sexual beings are likely to find that Aphrodite takes her revenge in ways they did not expect. The dualistic rejection of one aspect of God-given creation leads to tragedy and breakdown.

What we must do instead is to take the bold route. We must build temples to Jesus on territory at present occupied by Aphrodite. Many Christians may be shocked by this suggestion. What on earth might it mean in practice?

It means that we must learn, and practise, a genuinely Christian sexuality. The Bible joyfully celebrates God-given erotic love. The Song of Songs, again, is the obvious case in point; but the theme goes right back to Genesis 1 and 2 and right on, through the famous and symbolically powerful wedding at Cana in Galilee in the second chapter of John's gospel, to the marriage of Christ and the church in Revelation 21. But the Bible is also quite clear that sexual love is so important and powerful that it is vital to set it in its proper context. Electricity is important and powerful, but the child who sticks a paperclip into an electric socket to see the effect, or to get a thrill, will receive more than was bargained for. A record of Beethoven's symphonies is a wonderful thing, but it's no good trying to play it on equipment that's not ready for it. Sexuality is a powerful drive which needs a stable and appropriate setting if it is not to be potentially damaging and destructive. In common with many pastors and counsellors who repeatedly listen to tales of confusion and heartbreak on this score, I believe that having sexual relations outside marriage renders people less likely, not more likely, to be able to build and sustain a happy and successful permanent relationship within marriage itself. Memories of perplexing, painful or embarrassing situations all too easily return, and block the free and glad mutual self-giving which characterizes the full enjoyment of God-given sexuality.

This means that one of the most vital ways of building temples for Jesus on ground at present occupied by Aphrodite is to build and sustain Christian marriages. Instead of merely bemoaning the epidemic of divorces, the church should throw more energy into regular work with engaged and married couples, and with young people long before engagement, to help them to understand the true nature of our God-given maleness and femaleness and how they are designed to work together in partnership. If, as Paul insists in 2 Corinthians 4.13 — 5.5, our human bodies are to be enhanced, not destroyed, in the life to come, then they are valuable: what we do with them in the meantime matters.

At the same time, the church should also welcome and celebrate the lives of those who for whatever reason are called to celibacy. It is vital in today's climate of Aphrodite-worship that we affirm strongly a truth which is often forgotten today: that to live without sexual, by which I here mean genital, relationships is not to live a deprived or twisted life. Some celibates, of course, have simply repressed their sexuality in a dualistic and unhealthy way. Others, however, have taken it fully into account, and have learnt the secret of joyful self-control. St Paul insists in 1 Corinthians 7 that celibacy – in a world where it was almost unknown – is a valid and often important path for Christians to choose. If marriage symbolizes the coming together of heaven and earth (as in Revelation 21), celibacy is a powerful symbolic reminder that in the new creation, when death shall be no more, marriage as we know it will be irrelevant.

Either way, Christian marriage and Christian celibacy both raise the flag of the gospel where Aphrodite is worshipped. She will not be pleased; she may well strike back. Constant vigilance is required, but in exercising vigilance we must not marginalize sexuality, or pretend it isn't really there. Nor should we give the impression that Christians are against people enjoying themselves. It is by joyful and appropriate celebration that we will steal Aphrodite's thunder. Anything she can do, we can do better. What she promises, and fails to deliver, is the parody of what is promised, and delivered, when the sexual expression of human love occurs in the context for which it was made – the lifelong mutual commitment of one man and one woman.

It is in this context that we must insist, as a matter of basic Christian living, that the distortions of God-given sexuality which are so rampant in our society have no place in the life of the Christian. Excusing them in the name of tolerance, or in the name of affirming the goodness of sexuality itself, misses the point. It is *because* we affirm the goodness of sexuality that we must root out its distortions. As Paul says in Colossians 3.5, the distorted practices of a twisted sexuality are simply to be put to death. They belong to the area of idolatry, and have no part in Christian living.

But there are other ways, as well, in which we are to build temples for Jesus on territory occupied by Aphrodite. These may be riskier, but they demand serious consideration from churches in whose context it may be appropriate. Many of our cities have red-light areas where sexuality is 'celebrated' in a way which dehumanizes and degrades all who take part in it. The church must find ways of opposing the lucrative trade in Aphrodite-worship without denying the goodness and importance of sexuality itself. Indeed, it is precisely because we believe in the goodness and God-givenness of erotic love that we must show up its distortions and parodies for what they are. Churches working in or near red-light areas might consider buying or renting shop-fronts right in the middle of them, maybe even taking over premises at present used for the worship of the goddess, and establishing there a place of refuge for those who are battered, wounded, or scarred, emotionally or physically, by the abuse of sexuality. Open-air Eucharists in key locations might be another step forward. Such ventures will meet with resistance, and it is precisely here that churches involved in this work need the strength of full renewal to tackle the task with wisdom and courage. Aphrodite (often in league with Mammon) wields a lot of power in our society, and she will not give it up lightly. In addition, of course, the Internet has brought an astonishing and deeply disturbing range of possibilities for the exploitation of human sexuality. I suspect that only new legislation, properly enforced, will be able to deal with this fast-growing problem; and if that is the case the churches should be in the forefront of the campaign for such legislation. If we are called killjoys for our pains, so be it. Those who are caught in Aphrodite's trap, subject to the radical law of diminishing returns and the sense of shame and dehumanization which follows, will know that it is not we who are killing joy. That is precisely what the pagan deities do – which is why they are eager to accuse the church of the same thing.

Above all, and in line with my earlier insistence that the church must be for the world what Jesus was for Israel, it is vital that we in the church should come where there is real pain and dehumanization caused by the worship of Aphrodite, and be prepared to stand alongside those who are hurt, approaching them where they are, not where we want them to be. This will undoubtedly mean that Christians will find themselves, as Jesus found himself, at risk morally and physically. But let there be no mistake. Jesus did not shout platitudes at Israel from a safe distance. He identified with her plight, even though it cost him his life. The church must find appropriate ways of doing the same thing in the modern world.

Gaia

After three well-known pagan deities, we now come to Gaia, the earth-goddess. Nature-religions have always had their devotees. The rhythm of the seasons, the life of the earth, have always exercised a strong pull over human beings. Rightly so: we were made to live on this earth, to fit in with its cycles and basic order. But some urge us to recognize the earth itself as a goddess. They are going way beyond the instinct that makes May morning, and harvest festival, natural times of celebration.

Such apologists suggest that the earth is divine, and that this goddess has been suffering as a result of human mismanagement. We must therefore back off, allow Gaia to have her way, and find alternative ways of life which will give her her due. This explicit pantheism, which comes in many varieties, has gained ground with astonishing rapidity. The last time I gave a public lecture on Christian responsibility for the health of the natural world I was rebuked by two highly intelligent people who told me that humans should stop trying to fiddle with the system and let the earth look after itself.

What then is the proper Christian response to Gaia? The first time I ran into serious Gaia-theology – in the form of a well-written paperback at a friend's house – I was left with a strange and unpleasant feeling, almost like a bad taste in the mouth. Heavy-duty pantheism has a cloying, musty sense to it, as though one were abandoning the clarity of full human awareness and letting oneself slide into a world of mystery and incantation, of dark forces and feelings. The next morning, on my way to work, the feeling was still there. I called in for a short weekday service at my local parish church. I was slightly late, and Psalm 97 was being read as I came in. The response, which was being said at the end of every couple of verses, blew away the musty smell of pantheism with the fresh air of biblical truth: 'The Lord is King; the earth shall be glad thereof.' I realized at that moment that this is the truth of which Gaia-worship is the dark parody. There is one God, the creator; he loves his world and is active within it, but God and the world are emphatically not the same thing. The earth is glad when the Lord is King, not when Gaia exalts herself as Queen.

Ecological responsibility is a basic part of the major biblical and Christian tradition. What we find there is the call for humans to be responsible stewards of the world. Some have objected to the idea of 'stewardship', because it makes it sound as though humans are in some way exalted over the world. Some have gone further, and have objected to the very words 'King' and 'Kingdom', despite their biblical resonances: they have (it is claimed) encouraged exploitation and domination for so long that they are now too misleading to use. I respect those positions, but I do not share them. It seems to me a necessary part of the human vocation, from a Christian point of view, that we are called to wise, humble and responsible caretaking, looking after the good and beautiful world in which we live. We dare not downgrade humanness, as the pantheist does, in order to upgrade Gaia. We are not simply animals or plants. They – the animals and plants – need us to be *humans*, not to go on all fours (or grow roots) with them. The fact that the central biblical notion of Kingship has been abused by domineering humans is not in itself a reason to abandon the idea of the wise, loving, healing and judging sovereignty of the creator God. Jesus lived in a world where the most obvious 'kings' were people like the Herodian family and, of course, Caesar in Rome. But he went on talking about the kingdom of God. The horrible parodies must not rob us of the glorious reality.

The church, then, should take seriously the biblical perspective on creation. We must grasp firmly the role of humans as responsible agents, placed within creation to reflect the image of the creator, in love and care, upon it. And we must grasp the vision of the future held out in passages like Romans 8, 1 Corinthians 15, and Revelation 21—22. The earth will not be thrown away, jettisoned from the divine plan like so much trash. It will be filled with the glory of God, as the waters cover the sea. The fields will rejoice, and the trees will clap their hands. Our task in the meantime is to live in the light of that belief and that hope, and so to work out ways of glorifying the creator by bringing his healing love to the creation.

Many names, many gods

One of the most contentious issues in the modern Western church is the question of other faiths. Large-scale demographic movement has meant that many Christians in the Western world now have neighbours who are Muslims, Hindus, Sikhs or Buddhists. This has brought out into the open a debate which is often considered to be new, but which in fact goes back in its present form at least two hundred years. It was one of the major contentions of the Enlightenment that all religions were basically the same, and that the exalted place reserved in the West for Christianity was unwarranted. Fresh impetus has been given to this old idea by the way in which some unthinking would-be Christians have exploited, oppressed and even enslaved people of other religions; by the introduction of a religious dimension into the highly contentious debates about immigration, colour and culture in Western countries; and by the horrifying realization that, in the case of one religion in particular (Judaism), Christian language was used to cloak the paganism which committed one of the greatest public crimes of the last century – and that many Christians were taken in by it. In the light of all this, we have witnessed in the past decades a call for the recognition of the 'validity' of other religious faiths; for the abandonment of the attempt to evangelize those who profess them; and for the blending of different religious traditions into an explicitly syncretistic mix. The task of addressing this issue is fraught with problems, but something clearly must be said. There are two points which seem to me necessary at the start.

First, the belief that all religions are basically the same should be seen for what it is. It is an argument that all religious believers are really deists in disguise. This is what we should expect, granted the historical origins of the theory. It was promulgated originally by those who believed in a remote, detached god, who was only dimly reflected in the actual beliefs and religious practices of any humans, Christians included. Religion, within this scheme, consists only in general spiritual feelings, or in a sense of brotherhood or duty to all humankind. As a result, the specific things that Christians say about the god they worship are only vague approximations to reality. Once we boil them down to what they 'really' mean (and once we do the same with the rough-edged statements of other religions, too), then of course they will all look alike.

This idea, however, needs challenging. Claiming to dethrone religious arrogance, it is itself exceedingly arrogant, looking down from the assumed height of post-Enlightenment superiority on the poor benighted adherents of all the mainline religions, Christianity included. Claiming to disdain 'Western' religions, it is itself deeply wedded to one Western para-religion, namely, post-Enlightenment rationalist deism. It is not only deeply offensive to serious Christians, who believe that Jesus of Nazareth, and the Spirit of this Jesus, are the true and saving revelations of the creator of the world. It is also deeply offensive to mainline Jews and Muslims. It is somewhat easier for Hindus and Sikhs to believe, since their religions, themselves in some ways syncretistic, can more easily incorporate additions and modifications. But it does not accurately represent the belief or practice of any single known religion, except the intellectualized religious-ethical belief of some post-Enlightenment Westerners.

An alternative way of reaching a similar conclusion is to suggest that all religious persons are after all 'really' pantheists, or perhaps 'panentheists' (people who believe that everything is, if not God, then part of God). Here again we face the arrogance that claims to be able to reduce the religious experience of a wide range of people to one formulation, and then to use that formulation to criticize the account of the religion given by those who actually practise it. This cannot be the way forward.

Second, the Christian belief that Jesus is the Lord of the world – a belief for which many Christians have been prepared to die, rather than compromise, as they were urged to do, with bits of other religions – should not be confused with a belief in the superiority of Western culture. The majority of Christians in the world today do not live in the West, and the majority of Westerners neither profess nor practise Christianity. As an example of this, the average Anglican today is black, and does not speak English as a mother tongue.

It is an old trick to speak of Christianity as a 'Western' religion, thereby seeking to relativize or even discredit it. The West has sometimes arrogantly assumed that it was the main shareholder in Christianity Inc.; it has then further assumed that the supreme lordship of Jesus carries automatic cultural and (sometimes) racial superiority for all his followers. This extraordinary arrogance, of course, flies in the face of Jesus' rebuke to the pushy and power-hungry disciples, and contradicts the whole point of the gospel, that Jesus' supreme lordship is seen most clearly on the cross. And it is this arrogance that has provoked the rise of an apparently more humble relativism in our own day. But there is an opposite error. It is true that many Christians have mistakenly and disastrously transferred the biblical idea of Jesus' sole lordship to the sphere of the social or cultural claims of his contemporary followers. But relativism, equally mistakenly, transfers mutual cultural respect, which is proper to all inhabitants of the globe, to the claims that they make about the beings they worship.

This means, to put it bluntly, that the question of the sole lordship of Jesus is not a question about immigration policy. Indeed, if it is really *Jesus*, rather than a Western idol going under the same name, who is worshipped as Lord, then the church has every possible motivation to urge its surrounding society and culture to act with justice and generosity to maintain and enhance the dignity of all peoples and all races, whether on its own soil or elsewhere. To worship the creator God revealed in Jesus and by the Spirit is to be irrevocably committed to the worthiness of all who bear his image, and to the creation of communities in which all can live together in peace and mutual respect.

This means that Christians must gladly embrace the famous statement in John's gospel:

> 'I am the way,' replied Jesus, 'and the truth and the life! No one comes to the father except through me. If you had known me, you would have known my father. From now on you do know him! You have seen him!'   (John 14.6–7)

But Christians must also recognize that the only way in which this statement can be claimed is by those who are prepared to go, as Jesus went on the night he said those words, the way of the cross, the way of abnegation of power, the way of humility. To abuse a text like that by using it as a means to social or political power is to embrace an idolatry more dangerous than any we have examined in these chapters. But to marginalize such a text because of the danger of abuse is to abandon the garden because it might grow weeds. It is within the claim, and love, of Jesus that the solution may be found to all the problems of community and society that the relativist seeks to address.

The task of the church, faced with pluralism and relativism, is to give itself to the work that relativism at its best seeks to achieve, namely, the creation of a just and caring human community for all peoples, at both the global and the local level. There are many issues at many levels in which the church will find itself gladly affirming the values and aspirations of other households of faith, and we must not be shy about saying so. If we believe that Jesus really is Lord of the world, we must also believe that true human community will be created by following his agenda. The church must prove, by its deeds, that while relativism offers a lowest-common-denominator laissez-faire unity, there is a much richer prize on offer: a community in which all human beings are valued for who they are.

But not, necessarily, for what they worship. One feature of globalization is that we are able to see, close up, not only a wide variety of different human cultures but a wide variety of follies and dangers which those cultures produce. Christianity has been twisted in our own recent history into two dangerous idolatries: Nazism and Apartheid. Other religions are equally capable of doing the same thing. Hinduism's doctrine of karma has been much beloved by dilettante Westerners because it produced, by a different means, the 'tolerance' which post-Enlightenment thought prized above everything else. But this same doctrine insists that the untouchables be left as they are, that beggars dying in the street must continue to do so. Again, Islam has been welcomed by some Westerners because it, like Christianity, is a 'religion of the book'. But the books are somewhat different, to put it mildly; and adherence to them produces a different kind of discipleship. There are of course many varieties of Islam, as of Christianity. But central to the Muslim religion is the belief in a god who must be blindly obeyed, not in a god whose most profound self-revelation came through his being crucified. We are faced with the fact, sorely uncomfortable to Western religion, that if the Muslim Allah is the true god, then the crucified Jesus is a snare and a delusion; and vice versa. And this is not merely an abstract argument at the level of airy theology. It has to do with the nature of the communities that worship these beings. Sadly, the past thirty years have witnessed the rise of a militant Islam that was largely unknown to most modern Westerners until then; and the response from the Western powers – seen, inevitably, as 'Christians' by many in the Middle East – has given full proof that our culture has totally failed to understand the inner dynamics of how 'religions' actually work.

Let me give an example of what I mean. We in the Western world have long been, effectively, in a post-Christian society. But we have still kept the values of forgiveness, reconciliation, and new starts in human relationships as ideals. We may not practise them very successfully, but we still give them lip-service. But in many countries where there is no Christian tradition, forgiveness is seen as weakness. Reconciliation is regarded as folly. If someone offends or injures you, revenge is the proper, right, and entirely justified reaction. I am in no way extolling the modern West if I say that to live in societies like the latter, as I have for short periods, is deeply disturbing. There is more to religion than what humans do with their solitude.

Likewise, the very word 'salvation' itself means something different in different religions. For Judaism, it is inextricably bound up with the return to the land of Israel and the future coming of an as-yet-unknown Messiah. For Hinduism or Buddhism, it involves attaining a disembodied state in which the world of space and time is abandoned. But for Christians the promises about the land and the Messiah have already been summed up in Jesus; to deny this is to deny the very heart of the New Testament. And a disembodied state is the dualistic antithesis of the central Christian hope, expressed classically by Paul:

> At the present moment, you see, we are groaning, as we long to put on our heavenly building, in the belief that by putting it on we won't turn out to be naked. Yes: in the present 'tent', we groan under a great weight. But we don't want to put it off; we want to put on something else on top, so that what is doomed to die may be swallowed up with life.

> (2 Corinthians 5.2–4)

The whole point about the salvation offered by Jesus and the Spirit is that it is the reaffirmation of humanness, not its abolition. And this reaffirmation will include a re-embodying. 'Heaven' in early Christian thought is not the *final* resting-place of Christians: it is the place where, at the moment, God is preparing the new world, including the new bodies, that will at the end be brought into being in the marriage of the new heaven *with the new earth.* Such a vision of the future is the complete antithesis of that held in many world religions.

It is therefore imperative that Christians should not be browbeaten by the arrogance of the relativist into abandoning a Christlike and Christ-centred mission to all men, women and children. The adjectives are vital. Christian mission has often been anything but Christlike and Christ-centred. The church may well have a fair amount of repenting to do before it can say anything about Jesus that will not at once be invalidated by its own life and behaviour. But to wait for the church to be perfect before engaging in mission would be stupid. Reform will come as the church gives itself to the task.

The work of creating a just and peaceful human community is therefore the context in which a verbal message about Jesus can properly be spoken and heard. When the church is being for the world what Jesus was for Israel – welcoming the outcast, healing the sick, challenging the powers that oppress and enslave the poor – then its claim about Jesus will be self-authenticating. When we look around a church and see people of different ethnic origins being welcomed naturally and easily, without prejudice and without being patronized; when we find the church making a serious effort to accommodate within its styles of worship the different cultural traditions that are represented in such a congregation; then we will be seeing the church building shrines for the true God on ground at present firmly, and fiercely, occupied by the purveyors of pluralism and relativism.

Aphrodite, Gaia-worship and the generalized plurality of gods: each recognizes a particular truth about the way God has made the world, but then distorts it and, with it, the humans who are led into worshipping it. We have now looked at six areas where the church must build new shrines for Jesus. There are yet two more.

Questions for reflection or group discussion

1 (a) What signs are there of Aphrodite-worship in your community? How has the church responded, or how should it respond, to these?

   (b) How can the church be more effective in bearing witness to the revelation of God through the institution of marriage?

   (c) Sex is often big business (some of the richest people today are those who run the pornography and related industries). How can we be sure that we identify those who are actively propagating, and profiting from, the new idolatries, while coming to the rescue of those who, with whatever mixture of motives, are victims of them?

2 (a) How can we learn to value what is good in other religious traditions without compromising the gospel?

   (b) How can the gospel properly be brought to those of other faiths, particularly those who live in the neighbourhood of your church?

   (c) To what extent can Christians work alongside those with different faiths in the tasks they are to engage in?

13

New shrines for the true God (3)

We have now looked at five areas in which the church must combat paganism with the worship of Jesus. We must now look at two more, beginning with the style and mode of worship itself.

Pagan and Christian worship

Bacchus and the corn-kings

Among the nature-gods of ancient paganism were the gods of crops and vines, of food and drink. Bacchus, the god of wine, invited his devotees to celebrate in drunken revelry. Various corn-kings symbolized the annual dying of the seed and rising of the crop. Celebrating such gods often involved ritual meals in which it was believed that the worshippers partook of the god himself, and became equipped with his strength and power.

We have similar gods in our society today. There are those who make a religion of food and drink, if not in theory then certainly in practice. The results are everywhere apparent. Gourmet wining and dining for some, handfuls of rice for others. Heart attacks and cholesterol problems for some, distended bellies and empty outstretched hands for others. It doesn't take much common sense, or even much compassion, to see and to say that *this cannot be the way humans were meant to live.*

Enough has been written about the problem of world hunger. A certain amount – though not enough – has been done about it. One of the great strides forward in the past few years has been the recognition across the social and cultural spectrum in the Western world that the plight of the poor matters, and must impinge on our consciences more than it has done in the past. What we need now, though, is to see the full depth of the problem. If it were simply a matter of changing a few casual habits of life, that would be fairly easy. The fact that it is not easy at all shows that what is at stake is more than habit. We have worshipped at the shrine of Bacchus and the gods of the stomach, and they have now got a hold on us. How shall we break it?

Part at least of the answer is by celebrating the Christian festival of which Bacchic revels are the cruel and dehumanizing parody. The Eucharist, the breaking of bread and pouring out of wine, is precisely such a celebration. Jesus told us to celebrate this meal in his honour and memory. Paul wrote about it in terms which set its value very highly indeed: 'For whenever you eat this bread and drink the cup,' he said, 'you are announcing the Lord's death until he comes' (1 Corinthians 11.26). Writing in the context of his own denunciation of pagan worship in ultra-pagan Corinth, he deliberately uses apparently pagan language in speaking of those who eat the bread and drink the cup of the Lord becoming partakers, sharers, in the death of Jesus.

If he had done this today there would no doubt be some Christians who would think he was 'sailing close to the wind'. But, with the inner rationale of his thought secure, Paul knew that paganism was simply a distortion of the truth, and that one does not give up truth just because some people distort it. The Passover and other Old Testament festivals, and the Eucharist and other celebrations in the New, are the realities which Bacchus and the corn-kings are merely aping. To retreat from this claim is to let the pagan gods have it all their own way. To stake this claim properly, to celebrate the Eucharist with true joy and gratitude to the creator God for the goodness of creation and for redemption in Jesus, is to raise the flag of the Trinity, of the incarnate Jesus, precisely where at present pagan gods and goddesses are being worshipped. We must not underestimate the value of the regular celebration of this sacrament. At a time of rising paganism we need it as never before.

Let us, then, reject the rationalism that is suspicious of any sacramental action that cannot be analysed in a test-tube. Let us, too, reject the dualistic romanticism that believes that the only true religion has to do with what happens 'inwardly' rather than with outward or physical actions. The Eucharist is more than a bare memorial of Jesus' death. It is more than simply a 'visible word' (unless one is prepared to balance this by speaking of preaching as an 'audible sacrament'!). It is one of the moments in the life of God's people when all the lines of truth, faith, hope, love and service converge. At the Lord's table we become for a few moments what we truly are. We are in touch with reality, and are that much less likely to be deceived by man-made substitutes. Faced with a greedy and drunken world, we are called to celebrate in bread and wine the God who displaces any mere corn-king or Bacchus.

In particular, the Eucharist symbolically enacts a meal in which all partake on an equal footing. It is clear from 1 Corinthians 11 that the church was prone to let social and economic divisions appear in this context, destroying the sense of fellowship around the Lord's table. Such a travesty, and tragedy, is clearly to be avoided. On the contrary, in being ourselves fed by our Lord we pledge ourselves to share our bread with the hungry, not to snatch it all for ourselves.

It is possible, within regular worship and particularly within experimental services, to find ways of bringing this vividly to life. I remember one service at a time when we had all been made vividly aware of the plight of refugees and homeless people both in the UK and around the world. As we gathered around for the breaking of bread, I suggested that we take a pace back, making room between each pair of worshippers for silent, invisible guests to take their places as well. As it happened, we had read 1 Corinthians 15 as part of the liturgy, including the passage (verse 29) which speaks of people being baptized on behalf of the dead. I still have very little idea what that was all about, but if you can in principle be baptized on behalf of the dead, I do not see why you cannot receive Communion on behalf of the living. I invited each participant, in a time of silent prayer, to bring before God, as a guest at that table, one other person: a child orphaned by war; a young refugee widow, her baby at the breast; a grandmother who had lost home and family; a man returning home to find his entire village wiped out; a mother who had watched her children die of starvation. We brought them all, with tears and prayers and as rich a sense of fellowship as I can ever remember, into the presence of the living and loving Christ. And we left the building as different people.

Once we grasp the biblical theology of sacramental celebration we will find creative and imaginative ways of expressing it, and find ways of addressing the practical problems of (for instance) not having enough authorized people available to preside. If we do not do this, we will fill the vacuum with pseudo-sacramental actions of one sort or another which will express the gospel with less clarity. One of the great things about the Eucharist is that everyone can understand a celebratory meal. It speaks to every culture, and across every cultural boundary. It is therefore vital that we restore the Eucharist to its rightful place in our churches' life and worship.

Mantras, mysticism and prayer

What is true about the sacraments is also true of spirituality in general. We remarked in Chapter 9 on the rise of new movements in this area, which have liberated many Christians from stultifying practices which did them no good and only made them feel guilty. But at the same time there are many Christians who worry about some of the new movements. In particular, there are those who see the development of new ways of praying as a dangerous step in the direction of paganism. Some Christians are engaging in repetitive prayer, 'mantras', and the like, imitating some of the oriental religions in their practice of a prayer which goes beyond the range of consciousness, and attempts to commune with a god who is located in the depths of one's being. What are we to say to this?

There is such a thing as pagan prayer, and it is important not to be taken in by it. Christian prayer is always prayer *to* the transcendent creator God, not to the ground of our being or 'nature'. It is always made *through* Jesus Christ, who lived and died and rose again in history, not through some magic formula or mystic principle, divorced from this real Jesus. And it is made *in the power of* God's Holy Spirit, dwelling in the hearts of his people, not by means of an unknown force that takes control. Christian prayer, as Jesus said in the Sermon on the Mount (Matthew 6.7), is radically different from pagan prayer.

Likewise, Paul insists that in prayer it is good for the mind to be engaged. Speaking in tongues is fine, he says, but the mind must be given its due as well (1 Corinthians 14.6–19). But what many dualistic Christians fail to realize is that the God to whom we pray as Christians is not only the transcendent creator, not only the one revealed as the historical Jesus of Nazareth, but also the Spirit who dwells in our inmost depths, and longs to remake us and heal us in and from the deepest points of our humanness. Getting in touch with the Spirit during the course of this work is a mysterious business, and there may well be ways, superficially similar to some things practised in pagan prayer-habits, which are appropriate and indeed necessary in helping us truly to pray, as we are bidden, 'in the Spirit'.

Such prayer needs, in particular, to be open to things which cannot necessarily be reduced to words. Far too much modern Christian prayer has insisted on words, on logic, on getting everything clear and out into the open. This is of course important and indeed vital – as one aspect of the whole. But prayer, if it is to be Christian prayer, cannot be a grasping at control. It is precisely a *relinquishing* of control – to the one who is capable of doing far, far more than we can ask or imagine. It is saying '*Thy* will be done.' It is therefore appropriate, at some times and in some ways, that prayer should pass beyond the merely rational and wordy and engage with God, as Paul says in Romans 8, at a level too deep for words.

What are these ways?

Speaking in tongues may be one. Some Christians have found it to be the key which unlocks hidden depths they never knew existed.

Another way, much beloved of some and much suspected by others, is the way of silence. Some Christians in our portable-stereo society cannot exist without noise. Silence scares them. They can't control it. They need to hear voices always chattering, interrupting, commentating. But there are riches in true Christian silence which wordy Christians will never imagine. Silence, if properly used, can function like the warm dark earth in which the roots of the plant can grow, fruitful precisely in being undisturbed. There are ways in which God wishes to share his love with his people that quite simply cannot be put into words, and we impoverish ourselves if we ignore them.

A third way, explored in depth in the Eastern Orthodox tradition, is the way of the short repeated prayer. 'Lord Jesus Christ, Son of the Living God, have mercy on me, a sinner.' Said quietly over and over, like a mantra but with the all-important difference that this prayer concentrates the mind and heart on the historical person Jesus himself, this prayer can enable one to be still, to be humble, and then to hold the world, and those for whom one wishes to pray, in humble love before the Father who sent Jesus to be their Saviour as well as ours. Often, when we are unsure how to pray for someone, or for a situation, a repeated prayer like this can be a key which unlocks the door. And in doing so it is achieving what I am arguing for throughout these three chapters. It is showing forth the truth of which pagan prayer is a parody.

Idols of the mind

Paganism makes an appeal, not just to the body, as in Aphrodite-worship or Bacchic revelry, not just to the wallet, as in the worship of Mammon, but also to the mind. We have seen the modern academic university develop over the past two hundred years to the point where its latent dualism has become all too apparent. Scholars have pursued their own subjects in isolation from one another. Disciplines have become fragmented. The university has become, in effect, a *multiversity*; there is no sense of a shared vision, no united effort to understand and respond appropriately to the world in which we live. This is the world in which, for the most part, today's students find themselves.

In this situation a new monism will have a clear appeal. We have thrown away the old standards and goals which motivated our academic forefathers, the sense (for instance) that in studying the world of science we were thinking the creator's thoughts after him. What we are seeing instead is the rise of a new, essentially pagan, set of goals.

On the one hand, the universities are being used as wealth-creators. The paganism of materialism, of Mammon, Mars and the technological gods impinges at this point on the practice of scholarship: will the results of your research be profitable, in terms of hard cash, or won't they? Will the nuclear physics laboratory justify its existence in terms of new technology or military capability? But that is no way to probe the frontiers of knowledge. Academic standards are being sacrificed on the altar of financial or political expediency.

On the other hand, there are those who want to call all academic workers to submit to a 'politically correct' standard of social ethics, and to bend all their work in this direction. This movement, more apparent in the USA than in the UK, is equally stultifying to the proper practice of academic work. If it were not a serious problem, it would be almost comic to see how institutions that had carefully dismantled their older standards, had carefully stressed that they were no longer *in loco parentis*, and that the morals of their employees and their students were none of their business, are suddenly erecting new and quite rigid moralisms at the behest of powerful pressure groups. I once visited a university which had just issued a directive, in a country with hot summers, forbidding men to wear shorts, on the grounds that some women find them offensive. More seriously, many universities are experiencing campaigns to forbid a public hearing to people whose views are unwelcome to this or that group. Fortunately, many academic leaders see right through this: a university ought to be precisely a place where different arguments can be heard, weighed and judged on their merits. But in today's world we have witnessed a radical decline in 'reason' itself. Many people have already made up their minds about all the issues and simply want to impose them on everybody else. And when dictators and ideologues take over power, they introduce new languages, new codes. We should beware of all such moves. Despite their potential comic aspects, they frequently hide a strident paganism.

Once again, this is not something that should leave the Christian passive. He or she has a different agenda to work to. Many Christians have stressed for some time the importance of learning to think through one's academic subject from a Christian point of view. This was often difficult in the old dualistic environment: studying (say) chemistry simply didn't have many points of obvious contact with the Christian gospel, and to attempt to drag Christianity into an essay on monetarism or metallurgy was to look suspiciously like a fanatic. But it is now more imperative than ever that Christians, both in teaching and in learning positions, should make the effort to integrate their faith and their study. This means that the Christian student is called to work harder, perhaps, than might otherwise be necessary. We cannot and dare not cut corners, or settle for shallow agendas or cheap critiques. We need to think through the presuppositions and practice of our subjects, to explore their implications, and to work out prayerfully, and in collaboration with others, where the subject can and should be going for the glory of God and the good of his creation.

Prospects for the new shrines

We have now looked at seven areas in which, I have suggested, pagan forces of one kind or another have been at work in our society, and in which the church is called to build new shrines where the true God, the God revealed in Jesus and the Spirit, is to be worshipped instead. We must now address two all-important issues. First, how successful can we expect to be in this enterprise? Second, if the task is to be more than mere do-goodery, what other dimensions must it have?

How much may we expect to achieve? The question is not easy. I have argued that the agenda for the church must be based on the model 'As Jesus to Israel, so the church to the world.' But when Jesus engaged in his mission to Israel, it led him inexorably to the cross. Are Christians to work in the knowledge that they will incur the wrath of all around, and (if they do their job properly) will fail, and will end up being crucified, literally or metaphorically? Is this, perhaps, what Jesus meant when he told his disciples to take up their cross and follow him?

Another line of thought focuses on the resurrection. Jesus has won the decisive victory over the powers of evil. The resurrection inaugurates a new era. We do not have to win the victory all by ourselves. From now on the church can go out into the world with confidence, to *implement* the victory Jesus has already won. Is that the answer?

It seems to me that we have to hold both strands of thought together. Either without the other is misleading to the point of serious risk. But how can this be done?

From the very beginning of Christianity it was quite clear that the 'powers' were still active, and that any victory won over them on the cross still remained to be implemented. Persecution from Jews and pagans alike was the norm for the early church. Martyrdoms were frequent, and in fact for the first three centuries of the church's existence, and in many centuries after that as well, martyrdom became such a constant experience of Christianity that it was as much a regular discussion-point as 'signs and wonders', or the ordination of women, have been in the modern Western church. There was no suggestion that frequent martyrdoms meant that the church was failing. It was simply following in the way Jesus had led. It was, as Paul said in Colossians 1.24, filling up what was lacking in the sufferings of Christ. It was precisely in this period that the church was engaging in the head-on collision with paganism. And the church, despite muddle, setbacks, internal division and compromise, was winning victories. Churches were established, and grew, where before pagan deities were being worshipped. It seems that the old adage is true: the blood of the martyrs is the seed of the church.

The modern period is no different. The East African revivals of the early twentieth century took place in a context of great suffering, as various racially or tribally based governments attempted to establish their own rule and stamp out opposition, including that of Christians calling for justice. But the church has grown by leaps and bounds. Many Christians who lived under communist rule in Eastern Europe have emerged stronger, not weaker, for the experience. Indeed, if Western capitalists are tempted to regard the demise of communism as the vindication of their own way of life, it would be a good thing to ponder where the real victory lay. Many of the leaders in the struggle for liberation from communism were not advocates of capitalism. They were Christians, professing a belief which capitalism, too, has tried to ignore or squash. More recently we have seen terrible persecutions, and many martyrdoms, inflicted on the church by radical Islamists.

Suffering, then, is part of Christian living, and in paradoxical ways part of Christian victory. The 'success' of the projects I have been advocating will never be measured simply in statistics. If we measure success in normal modern Western terms, there will always be some churches that feel themselves to be failing. True success will never be a matter of a triumphalist Christianity taking over from a cowed paganism. On the contrary, it will come as Jesus' victory came: in the blind seeing, the deaf hearing, and the poor receiving good news. And the messengers, or some of them, will bear the shame and the scorn, and sometimes the physical violence, that will come about when 'normal' ways of doing things – which increasingly means pagan ways of doing things – are challenged. Some who attempt the programme I have suggested will not get the promotion they expected and deserved in their jobs. Some will receive hate-mail and threats. Some will incur physical violence. There will be real victories, but they will come in the context of real suffering.

But at the same time the Christian tradition insists that following in the way of Christ is not simply a matter of endlessly repeating a pattern (particularly, a pattern of 'failing'!) of which Jesus was merely the first representative. It was the great insight of the Protestant reformers that what was done on the cross was done *once for all*, unrepeatably. What Jesus achieved was not merely to set an example of the way things always are and always will be. He brought about a decisive change in the balance of spiritual power in the cosmos. Nothing can be the same after that.

The Christian goes about the new tasks, therefore, with a humble and cross-centred confidence. It is a confidence that is the very opposite of arrogance. It presupposes a clear recognition of one's own unworthiness. It is given a sense of direction by nothing else than the love of God, to be shared with the world. It has as its working model the self-giving love of Jesus going to the cross. It is tempered all along with the knowledge that anything which is 'achieved' in this work is to be attributed not to one's own skill, wisdom, labour or effort, but to the Spirit of the living God himself. It recognizes that all Christian 'achievements' in this life are shot through with ambiguity, but that at the same time they anticipate, and gain their significance from, the great coming day when the kingdom will finally be established. It is impossible to justify churches that really are failing, failing in their witness to a pagan society, on the grounds that failure is what Christianity is all about. There are grounds for confidence and hope, but for a confidence and hope that have humility as their constant companion.

All of this is summed up in the passage which Paul wrote as the climax of one central argument in the letter to the Romans:

> We know, in fact, that God works all things together for good to
> those who love him, who are called according to his purpose ...
>
> What then shall we say to all this?
> If God is for us, who is against us?
> God, after all, did not spare his own son; he gave him up for
>   us all!
> How then will he not, with him, freely give all things to us?
> Who will bring a charge against God's chosen ones?
> It is God who declares them in the right.
> Who is going to condemn?
> It is the Messiah, Jesus, who has died, or rather has been raised;
> who is at God's right hand, and who also prays on our behalf!
> Who shall separate us from the Messiah's love?
> Suffering, or hardship, or persecution, or famine, or naked-
>   ness, or danger, or sword? As the Bible says,
>
> Because of you we are being killed all day long;
> We are regarded as sheep destined for slaughter.
>
> No: in all these things we are completely victorious through the
> one who loved us.   (Romans 8.28, 31–37)

Here is a model of Christian work in the world. Confidence in the love of God disclosed through Jesus and the Spirit, and in that alone; facing persecution and suffering as a result, yet knowing that victory is both already won and certainly to be won in the future; and celebrating, in language borrowed from the picture of God's Servant in Isaiah 50, the constant help of the living God even when all seems in vain. No wonder Paul concludes the chapter as he does:

> I am persuaded, you see, that neither death nor life, nor angels nor rulers, nor the present, nor the future, nor powers, nor height, nor depth, nor any other creature will be able to separate us from the love of God in King Jesus our Lord.
>
> (Romans 8.38–39)

It is the same vision which we find in the farewell discourses of John's gospel. Jesus, looking ahead to his leaving the disciples and returning to them in the resurrection and the gift of the Spirit, speaks of their proper blend of pain and joy: 'You have sorrow now. But I shall see you again, and your hearts will celebrate, and nobody will take your celebration away from you' (John 16.22). Here is the authentically Christian note. Sorrow and joy, pain and victory are not opposites in the Christian life. They go hand in hand. We can indeed expect victory, but it will always be paradoxical. Any other expectation will lead us astray.

Paganism and spiritual warfare

In the same letter in which he speaks of the great victory of Christ over all the powers that ever were (Ephesians 1.20–23), Paul also writes of the spiritual battle which the church must engage in if she is to implement that victory in the world (6.10–20). It is right that we should close these three chapters on this note, lest any should imagine that the task can be reduced simply to the level of church leaders suggesting, and church committees planning, new programmes. Paul writes:

> What else is there to say? Just this: be strong in the Lord, and in the strength of his power. Put on God's complete armour. Then you'll be able to stand firm against the devil's trickery. The warfare we're engaged in, you see, isn't against flesh and blood. It's against the leaders, against the authorities, against the powers

that rule the world in this dark age, against the wicked spiritual elements in the heavenly places.

For this reason, you must take up God's complete armour. Then, when wickedness grabs its moment, you'll be able to withstand, to do what needs to be done, and still to be on your feet when it's all over. So stand firm! Put the belt of truth round your waist; put on justice as your breastplate; for shoes on your feet, ready for battle, take the good news of peace. With it all, take the shield of faith; if you've got that, you'll be able to quench all the flaming arrows of the evil one. Take the helmet of salvation, and the sword of the spirit, which is God's word.

Pray on every occasion in the spirit, with every type of prayer and intercession. You'll need to keep awake and alert for this, with all perseverance and intercession for all God's holy ones – and also for me! Please pray that God will give me his words to speak when I open my mouth, so that I can make known, loud and clear, the secret truth of the gospel. That, after all, is why I'm a chained-up ambassador! Pray that I may announce it boldly; that's what I'm duty-bound to do.

(Ephesians 6.10–20)

Paul's extended metaphor of a soldier's armour may worry some who have become sensitive to the problem of Mars-worship in our society. But it reflects the reality which some, in rejecting old dualisms, are unwilling to face. There is such a thing as supra-human evil, and to challenge it will engage the Christian not just in thinking and acting but in what we can only call spiritual warfare. Paul offers the Christian the necessary defence, and the necessary weapons, to go about the task.

We need to take seriously each piece of armour which Paul lists, and particularly the last. He puts prayer over all. The constant loving contact between the Christian and the creator, between the believer and the Lord, between Christ's soldier and Christ's Spirit – for this there is no substitute. There is a God who is stronger than all the pagan powers, and this God is made known as Father, Son and Spirit. This God equips his people with the protection and the power that they need, if only they will stay close to him and invoke his love and grace. It is all available, in prayer and sacrament, as we go about his work of making known his love and his power. We go to God's tasks, secure in God's keeping.

Questions for reflection or group discussion

1 (a) Go back through the renewals described in Chapters 9 and 10. How, specifically, do these various renewals prepare the church for the tasks outlined in Chapters 11, 12 and 13?

   (b) Are you aware of other renewals, and other paganisms, that are not mentioned here? How would you fit them into the developing pattern?

2 (a) How can we be sure that we are attempting the new tasks in Jesus' way, not simply rushing at them with our own hidden agendas and in our own style?

   (b) How can we strike the right balance between 'prayer' and 'action'? To which are you more naturally inclined?

3 (a) Have you, as an individual or a church, experienced suffering of any sort which you can in any way connect with your attempt to live and work for God in the world?

   (b) If the answer to this is clearly 'no', what might that say about the impact of the church on its surrounding culture?

   (c) How can we support other Christians, in this country or elsewhere, who are experiencing suffering because of their faith?

14

The two-edged sword

We have now set out several ways in which God has been renewing his church, and several new tasks to which we are called. But one question still presses. Do these tasks have anything to do with 'preaching the gospel'?

The great divide

It is commonly thought that there is a gulf between two different sorts of task that Christians engage in. On the one hand there is 'preaching the gospel', by which is meant issuing an invitation to individuals to put their trust in Jesus as Saviour and Lord, and to discover, through personal relationship with him, a new dimension to life here and a new hope for life hereafter. On the other hand there is 'social action', the attempt to apply the message of Jesus to society and the world. These have sometimes been categorized as 'evangelism' and 'mission' respectively. Some who accept this great divide may well have thought that what I have been advocating in the previous two chapters belongs in the 'social action' or 'mission' category.

Perhaps I can explain from personal experience why I think this divide is highly misleading.

In much of my early life as a Christian I was taught, sometimes explicitly and usually by implication, that one should not mix up evangelism and the pursuit of social justice. The former worked at the vertical dimension, the relationship between God and humans; the latter at the horizontal, the relationship humans have with one another. In addition, I learned, it was easy to show that when churches had concentrated on the latter, they had stopped emphasizing the former. Since evangelism has to do with the eternal state of human beings, and social justice only with their temporary existence in this world, it should be clear where the priorities ought to lie. There is no point in oiling the engine of a car that is about to plunge over a cliff. Much better prepare the passengers for a more certain and secure future the other side of death.

I remember quite vividly living within this mindset myself. On one occasion I recall taking the chair at a seminar in which the speaker – a theologian who was also a politician – was expounding a holistic view of evangelism and social justice. I simply could not understand how he was putting the two together. More disconcerting still, when I asked him how he was doing it, *he did not understand my question.* For him the two things were part of the same whole. For me they belonged in completely different worlds.

The thing that began to change my mind was working through Paul's letter to the church in Colossae. As I wrestled with the great poem in the first chapter (1.15–20), I found a view of Christ as the Lord of all the powers that ever existed. At the same time, I was coming to terms with perplexities in my own life, things for which the gentle dualisms of my background had not prepared me. The upshot was that by the time I had finished with Colossians (or rather, by the time it had finished with me) I not only understood where that seminar speaker had been coming from: I now had difficulty understanding how I had failed to see the point myself. And in the light of this new point of view, a great deal in the gospels and epistles (not to mention other parts of the Bible) which I had formerly not grasped began to make sense.

The roots of the divide

I now see that what I had taken to be a biblical division between 'the gospel' and 'social justice' has its roots, not in the Bible, but rather in non-biblical philosophical traditions which we mentioned in Chapter 1. In the eighteenth century, the philosopher G. E. Lessing spoke of a 'great ugly ditch' between the eternal truths of reason and the contingent truths of space–time reality. You can't mix the two, he said: and two centuries have blindly followed him into this radical dualism, including Christians convinced that in doing so they were being 'biblical'.

But what we find in the Bible is precisely that mixture which Lessing declared impossible. God called Abraham in order to undo the problem of Adam, and of Babel. But Babel is not to be undone by God declaring that the space–time universe is to be obliterated altogether, and that some people are called to belong to a new 'spiritual' world. God has chosen to work *within* space–time reality, not to abolish or ignore it. Again, God's call to Israel to be a holy people emphatically involved a call to justice in their society, as the prophets never tired of reminding them. Justice in community, and the knowledge and worship of God, are seen as two parts of the same indivisible whole (see, for example, Jeremiah 22.15–16). And God's call through John the Baptist seems to have involved urging people not only to escape the coming judgment but also to put their houses in order in the present time (Luke 3.7–14).

What about Jesus? The popular picture of Jesus is of his preaching a timeless gospel in which the 'spiritual' dimension of life was emphasized, leaving on one side the social or political troubles which pressed on his contemporaries. As we saw in the first half of this book, that is a dangerous half-truth, which blunts the cutting edge of the whole gospel. It was certainly not the view of Paul, who was run out of town on one occasion for announcing that there was 'another king', and who summoned the Philippian church, living as they were in a proud Roman colony, to acknowledge that Jesus alone was Lord – in other words, that Caesar wasn't.

The roots of the split between 'evangelism' and 'social action' are not as deep within the Christian tradition as is often thought. Indeed, it could be argued that the split came about because of the failure of the church to work out the problems inherent in its own holistic claim. The wars of religion that bedevilled Europe from the sixteenth century onwards (in which, as in the crusades, theological motives were invented to legitimate wars whose real reasons lay elsewhere) produced a generation that was understandably sickened by the sight of people killing one another in the name of the Prince of Peace. And this gave a strong impetus to the Enlightenment. If religion is such a nuisance, we will banish it to a private, abstract sphere, where it will no longer cause war and political squabbling; and we will organize our lives in a civilized fashion, in rational and sensible (but not theological) ways. This, I suggest, is the view that we have inherited from the past two centuries; that many confuse with Christianity itself; and that is now reaching its dying gasps with the rise of the neo-paganisms that we have been studying.

Towards a complete gospel

Jesus urged his contemporaries to 'repent and believe the gospel'. Most churchgoing people today would reckon they knew what he meant: tell God you are sorry for your private sins, and entrust your-self, for your eternal salvation, to the mercy of God as revealed in Jesus. But would his contemporaries have understood that as the force of his summons? I think not.

In the autobiography of the Jewish writer Josephus, a younger contemporary of St Paul, there is a remarkable parallel to these words of Jesus. Josephus is describing his actions as a would-be peacemaker between Rome and the Jewish rebels. He was in command of a force in Galilee in AD 66, and had the task of confronting a group of rebels (led, interestingly enough, by someone called Jesus the Galilean!). His message to this group, and to its leader in particular, was simple: they should *repent, and believe in him* (Josephus, *Life*, 110; cf. 17, 167, 262). The words in Greek are virtually the same as those used in the gospels (e.g. Mark 1.15). Now Josephus clearly had no thought of a 'spiritual' repentance, or merely a turning from private sins; nor did trusting in him, Josephus, involve the sort of 'faith' that, from Paul at least, came to be associated with trust in Jesus. Josephus was talking about his message to the rebels: give up your way of being Israel, your attempt to fight God's battles in your own style, and instead put your trust in the programme that I am trying to implement.

Some will no doubt object that this parallel is illegitimate. I submit that it needs to be taken extremely seriously. Here we have a description of events taking place at a time when the gospels were being written, and concerning groups of dissident Jews in exactly the same part of the country as had been frequented by the Jesus of the gospels. Of course there are differences. The whole thrust of the gospels' story of Jesus is radically different from that of Josephus' autobiography. But whatever other dimensions we wish to include in our reading of Jesus' command to repent and believe the gospel, we cannot avoid this one: that the command involves a summons to abandon other ways of being Israel, other ways of being human, and to trust instead in Jesus' way, Jesus' agenda, Jesus' path. It is, in fact, an encapsulated form of the challenge which Israel was supposed to be offering to the world: stop following your idolatrous lifestyle, and join us in wor-shipping the true God, the creator. Now, however, it is being offered *to* Israel by one who was claiming to act as the true Israel, claiming, as we have already seen, to embody Israel's destiny in himself.

I suggest, therefore, that right from the start the summons of the Christian gospel was not a purely 'spiritual' message about an eternal salvation, any more than it was an appeal only for a pragmatic social reformation. The summons is a call to abandon idols and follow the living God. This involves *both* the invitation to discover, in Jesus, the true rescue from sin and death (the worship of idols, and the result of that worship) *and* the summons to follow Jesus instead in a new way of life in which idolatry is eschewed at every level and through which the healing love of the creator can reach out to his world. The power of the idols was broken at the cross, and those who embrace the cross as the centre of their worship are embracing their own liberation from the idolatries that have imprisoned and dehumanized them.

Jesus is Lord

This, of course, is the great truth which Christians celebrate in the Ascension. Jesus is exalted as the Lord of the cosmos, supreme over all the powers. It is Jesus' Ascension, in particular, that launches the church on its mission. When the disciples asked Jesus, 'Master, is this the time when you are going to restore the kingdom to Israel?' (Acts 1.6), it is commonly assumed that Jesus' answer meant 'No'. What he said was, 'It's not your business to know about times and dates . . . The Father has placed all that under his own direct authority. What will happen, though, is that you will receive power when the Holy Spirit comes upon you. Then you shall be my witnesses . . . to the very end of the earth' (Acts 1.7–8, compare Matthew 28.16–20). In fact, I suggest that this answer was a redefined 'Yes'. In sending his disciples out (they were careful, at once, to restore their number to the symbolic twelve), Jesus *was* restoring the kingdom to Israel: but it was Israel as redefined by his death and resurrection. The Ascension launches the church, not on a nationalist or triumphalist mission, but on the task of announcing and inaugurating the sovereign rule of *Jesus* in the whole world.

This is the fulfilment of the vision of Daniel, in which the Son of Man is exalted to sit beside the Ancient of Days, the creator himself (Daniel 7.9–14). (The 'coming' of the Son of Man, it should be noted, is a coming *to God* in vindication and glory, not a 'return' to earth. The second coming of Jesus is established on quite other grounds and texts.) Jesus ascends as the representative of Israel, who all along was called to be the people through whom the creator would establish his wise and healing rule over the world. As we saw in Chapter 7, the victory of Jesus is the climactic moment in the story of the human race, of Israel, and even of God himself.

If Jesus is Lord, and if the gospel consists of the effective announcement of this fact to the world, there can be no division between the different sorts of tasks that follow. Any gospel which does not embrace both 'evangelism' and 'social action' is a counterfeit, offering either an escapist's dream, which leaves the power structures of the world untouched, or a mere social reform which leaves the soaring spiritual dimension of reality out of consideration, and thereby dooms itself to compromise and failure.

The problem of a counterfeit gospel is not a new one. St Paul addressed it in one of his sharpest letters, that to the Galatians. This book is often read as a defence of the 'Protestant gospel', which understands the message of justification by faith as a charter of individual salvation, by faith in Jesus and the cross rather than by doing good works. But such a reading emasculates the letter (which is not in fact about 'salvation' at all; the word never occurs there). Paul is attacking the attempt to confine grace to one ethnic group. The all-important issue is: 'Must I become a Jew in order to belong to the true people of God?' And this reflects the deepest question of all: what does it mean to worship the true God? In Galatians 4.1–11 he shows that the true God – the God revealed as Father, Son and Spirit – has broken the rule of the 'powers'. And he demonstrates that if the Galatians, or anyone else, allow the power structures of the world to remain intact, as they will do if they continue to uphold the Jew/Gentile division within the church, they are embracing a non-gospel. In such a message, there is no real good news: the cross has not won the victory over the powers. They still rule supreme.

For Paul, 'justification by faith' is not simply a message about how individuals may find peace with God. It is a message about how God is calling for himself a people who are both the objects of his special love and the instruments through whom he will extend that love to the world. It insists that this company of people is characterized not by its membership in a particular race, a particular gender, a particular social class (Galatians 3.28) but simply by faith in Jesus. (The 'works of the law' of which Paul writes disparagingly are *not* human achievements of moral self-effort, still less the God-given attempt to work for justice in society, but obedience to specific commands of the Jewish law, designed to show that one belongs to the ethnic family of Abraham.) *The message, at this level, is simple: all who believe in Jesus belong to the same family and should be eating at the same table.* That is what Paul's doctrine of justification is all about. It is ironic that a doctrine designed to unite Christians from different backgrounds has so often been used as a means of dividing them. It is even more ironic that a doctrine which originated in the struggle against the principalities and powers should so often be used as a watchword against 'corrupting' the gospel by involving it with just such issues. These are ironies we can do without.

'Justification', then, is not a doctrine about 'how to become a Christian'. It is about how to *recognize* that someone *has become* a Christian – a very different thing. Richard Hooker, the great Anglican theologian of the Elizabethan period, argued strongly and truly that one is not justified by believing in justification by faith. One is justified *by faith* – that is, faith in Jesus. And it is to such faith that the gospel summons men, women and children. What will such faith involve?

Let there be no mistake. To proclaim the lordship of Jesus in all the world can never be a matter of merely inviting people to embrace a personal salvation which leaves the power structures of the world untouched. If it is reduced to that, then in the name of the whole New Testament we must say that the Jesus of whom such a message speaks is not Jesus of Nazareth, but an idol who has usurped his name and distorted his message. And at the same time we must say that to work for justice and peace in the world on any basis other than the declaration that the crucified and risen Jesus is Lord of the world, and that his Spirit is at work today to implement his victory, is to fight idolatry with idolatry. Only Jesus, the real Jesus, is Lord; only by his Spirit is there victory, is there hope. The gospel promises the life of the age to come, the hope of resurrection, to all who turn from idols and trust in this Jesus. The same gospel promises that, because his victorious reign has already begun, the power of his self-giving love can challenge and dethrone the usurping idols that still enslave, distort and destroy human life. There is one gospel, because there is 'one body and one Spirit . . . one hope of your calling, one Lord, one faith, one baptism, one God and Father of all' (Ephesians 4.4–6). There is one world, one God, one gospel. And with this gospel we, however surprisingly, have been entrusted. We are not spectators in this drama. We ourselves are summoned to be God's agents in bringing this earth-shattering message to the world – and to the church! – that so desperately needs it.

If all this is true, there is one final question. Who is this God that we worship? How can we use words which will begin to do justice to the truth that we celebrate in worship and announce to the world?

Questions for reflection or group discussion

1 (a) Is your church better at 'evangelism' or 'mission'? Or does it find difficulty with both? If so, why? Where could you begin to make some inroads into the task?

2 (a) Why has there been so much acceptance in the church of the split between 'evangelism' and 'mission'?
 (b) What lessons can we draw from Jesus' own integrated proclamation of the gospel?

15

The God we confess

If Christians seek to engage in the great tasks now before them, they need renewing in one way in particular: in their vision of God himself. When the early church found itself battling with paganism, the question at the heart of it all was: who is God? It was in response to this that the doctrine of the Trinity emerged. Why?

The growth of a vision

When I was younger, I could never understand why St Patrick needed to use a shamrock to evangelize the Irish. I had never heard an evangelistic sermon which expounded the doctrine of the Trinity, and I couldn't see why one would want to try. It makes a lot more sense to me now. Patrick could not assume, and we cannot today assume, that people know what Christians mean when we say 'God'. If we want to tell them of a God who is out there and in here, of a God who is supremely holy and good and yet who took evil into himself and dealt with it, we will need more than just shamrocks.

Belief in the Trinity is not just putting a mental tick beside a doctrine, agreeing with its correctness at a purely intellectual level. This belief was hammered out in learned debate, yes; it was also tested out in the agony of the Roman arenas. It was this view of God which the early Christians found themselves compelled to articulate as they were facing the might of paganism. God's answer to the arrogance and chaos of Babel (Genesis 11) was the call of Abraham and, from Abraham's point of view, the embracing of monotheism. God's answer to the arrogance and chaos of paganism two thousand years ago was to develop his self-revelation to Abraham so that it became the full revelation of himself as Father, Son and Spirit.

The words the early fathers used to express this doctrine ('substance', 'nature', 'person' and so forth) are not to be cast in stone. Anyone who really believes that God exists in three *persons*, in the modern English sense of 'person', probably believes that there are three gods. What matters is what the fathers were using these words to express. They were not trying to produce scholars' formulae to baffle the unlearned, or philosophical puzzles to appeal to pagans on their own terms. Nor were they providing an arcane mystery to be grasped only by initiates. They grasped the central truth of the New Testament, and did their best to communicate it to their contemporaries. We in our turn can do no less.

The theologians who worked out this doctrine have regularly been criticized in recent years. They have been accused of transforming the gospel from the simple message of Jesus to a Greek philosophical nightmare. It has become wearyingly commonplace to hear clergy say, as they approach Trinity Sunday, that they can't make head or tail of all that stuff and they know their people can't either. That, I suspect, is because some time ago the church gave up its basic task of addressing the pagan world with the news about the God whom paganism parodies, and lapsed instead into one of various sub-Christian alternative views of the task, and thus views of God. Those who criticize the fathers regard themselves as plain, uncomplicated people; but actually the gibes reflect quite a complex agenda, consisting of Enlightenment categories that are now beginning to look increasingly threadbare.

Christians of a more conservative stamp regularly give adherence to the doctrine of the Trinity, but it often plays a minimal role in their thinking (in fact, it might challenge a certain amount of it). For some conservative Protestants, the doctrine is a symptom of whether one believes the Bible, which is presumed to teach this doctrine. For some conservative Catholics, it is a test of whether one will accept church tradition, whether or not they can make any sense of it. But, again, we cannot rest content with such positions when faced with our new tasks. How are we to re-appropriate the fact that the early fathers were trying to express?

Speaking truly of God

The problem, I think, is not just that the technical terms of early theological debate have ceased to be in common currency, so that people hear the old words and respond with either unthinking lip-service or thinking incredulity. The problem is that people in the modern Western world have come to regard the word 'God', or even 'god', as univocal. They assume that it means only one thing, and that all users of the word mean the same thing by it. If you are challenged on the street with the question 'Do you believe in God?' (a question more likely, these days, to come from a pollster than a preacher), it is assumed that we all know what is being spoken of. To reply, 'Which God?' would probably throw the questioner, let alone the statistics, into confusion.

But that is surely the only proper reply. We have seen that a great many gods are regularly worshipped in our society. Among them we still find the old god of deist belief: the distant, remote, spy-in-the-sky sort of god. He might perhaps have had a hand in the creation of the world, though he may have delegated this job to abstract forces in which he took little interest. He might or might not have had a rather close relationship with Jesus. He might, but probably might not, take much interest in individuals and society today. When people tell me, as they often do, that they don't believe in God, as often as not I discover on further enquiry that *this is the God they don't believe in.* Then comes the surprise (to them): *nor do I.* I believe in the God of the Bible, and the more I learn about him the more I find that there are three things which are to be said about him, and that the old words of Father, Son and Spirit come as close to hitting the nail on the head as anything else I have yet heard.

There are those who claim that this doctrine is not in fact biblical. This is far too large an issue to explore fully in this book, but I believe the charge to be quite mistaken. It is true that the biblical writers never use the detailed theological language that the fathers employed. But they set the agenda which the fathers were following. Indeed, if we read passages like Galatians 4.1–11, Romans 8.1–11, John 14—16, John 20, and a whole lot more we may well find ourselves driven to say that if the early fathers, and the doctrine of the Trinity, had not existed, it would have been necessary to invent them. If they hadn't done the job, we would have had to do it from scratch ourselves.

I remember Bishop Stephen Neill once saying that Christology is a doctrine about God, and the Trinity is a doctrine about Jesus. There is a vital truth at the heart of this apparent paradox. It is in looking at Jesus that we discover who God really is. But if we are to keep focused on Jesus and still talk about God, we must make distinctions, on the one hand, between Jesus and the creator God, and, on the other hand, between the human Jesus and the Spirit who indwells God's people. What happens when we explore these distinctions?

In focusing on Jesus, we discover again and again that God is not a dualist's god. He is the creator of the universe. But we also discover – and it continues to burst upon us as a surprise – that this creator has expressed his love in person, by sharing our human life, and by dying as the focal point of Israel, the race chosen to be the means of saving the world. The creator loves us *that much*. Only a vision of God which keeps the crucified and risen Jesus absolutely central can even begin to keep hold of this astonishing truth. Dualism, paganism, deism, relativism – nothing can compete with this.

But the vision of God which thus comes into focus needs a final element, and receives it at the feast of Pentecost. The Jews developed several ways of speaking of the creator as being active and alive to heal and renew his world from within. They talked of God's Word, his Presence, his Wisdom, his Spirit, personifying various seemingly abstract or quasi-physical entities as though they were almost independent realities. At the same time, they maintained their firm hold on the One God. Christianity, not surprisingly, applied some of this language to Jesus: he is God's Word, God's Wisdom. But the early Christians, soon after Jesus' Ascension, began to experience God in a way previously only known in very limited circles, particularly among prophets and other great leaders of God's people. They experienced God living within them, coming upon them like a new wind given to be their own breath, like a fire which burnt without consuming them. And this new life was stamped with a recognizable character. It was the life of Jesus himself. The risen Jesus had gone from their sight; but, as he had promised, a wind from God came and took possession of them, and they knew that this wind, or breath, or Spirit (in Greek or Aramaic the words are the same), was the living presence of the living God, the God they had come to see most clearly in Jesus. 'I will ask the Father,' said Jesus, 'and he will give you another helper, to be with you for ever. This other helper is the spirit of truth. The world can't receive him, because it doesn't see him or know him. But you know him, because he lives with you, and will be in you.' (John 14.16–17).

For the early Christians to speak, therefore, of a threeness about their knowledge of this One God was in no way, as is sometimes casually asserted, to lapse into paganism. It was to build solidly on centuries of Jewish thought about the One God and his relationship with his world, and to claim that the hope and faith of Israel had now been fulfilled in Jesus, and was being implemented by the Spirit. The one true God, the creator, had always been active in his world, and had spoken through Israel's prophets to call the nation to be the light of the world. Now, in Jesus, the creator himself had come in person to fulfil Israel's destiny. Now, in the Spirit, the creator/redeemer God was coming to live in his people, to enable them to believe in Jesus, and to be his witnesses, summoning his world to abandon idols and find liberation and life in worshipping him instead.

Certain passages, in Paul in particular, point so clearly in the direction of Trinitarian theology that I find it impossible to believe that he did not realize what he was saying. Thus, for instance, when he writes to Corinth he is faced with a background of paganism in which different 'spirits' would 'possess' people. Against this, he is arguing forcibly that the variety within Christian spiritual experience is to be held together within a single unity. He is precisely asserting Jewish-style monotheism over against pagan polytheism. Yet within this very argument his crucial phrase is threefold: there are varieties of gifts, but the same Spirit; varieties of ministries, but the same Lord; varieties of working, but the same God is working all in everyone (1 Corinthians 12.4–6). This, I submit, is typical of the often understated but very powerful Trinitarian thought of the New Testament as a whole. When one is faced with paganism, and trying to speak the truth about the creator of the universe, one will be forced again and again to speak of oneness and threeness. And the threeness comes out again and again in forms like these: God, Lord, Spirit; Father, Son, Spirit; God, Jesus, Spirit; Creator, Word, Breath. That is why, when we reach Pentecost within the church's calendar, we have a sense that the picture is now complete.

The Trinity: the essential equipment for the task

The whole thrust of this book is that the true God has, in Jesus, dethroned the false gods, and that, by his Spirit at work in and through his people, he is implementing that victory in the world today. But worshipping this true God, and indeed believing in him, is not easy. It is like keeping on course on a mountain walk through thick mist and a swirling wind. We need to check the compass continually if we are to keep our bearings. How do we do this, and what do we find when we do?

The check on the compass is always Jesus himself. We cannot know the gospels too well. There is always more to ponder, more to discover, more that will challenge our comfortable assumptions and our cosy semi-idolatries. We are always liable to be blown off course, but a close and continuous study of, and meditation upon, Jesus will provide the stabilizing factor we need. It is in the light of him that we go on rediscovering who the creator of the universe really is; it is in the light of him that we go on rediscovering who the Spirit is, and distinguishing his Spirit from the other spirits that present themselves to us from time to time.

I mentioned St Patrick earlier; and in our last chapter we looked at the Christian armour commended by St Paul. Look now at the 'breastplate' that Patrick chose to wear as he confronted age-old paganism with the news of the God of love revealed in the cross. Notice not least how he focuses so clearly, in the second stanza, on the events of Jesus' life which we have traced in this book; and how, in the third stanza, he takes over the territory that paganism had made its own, and claims it for the Triune God:

I bind unto myself this day the strong name of the Trinity;
By invocation of the same, the three in one and one in three.
Of whom all nature hath creation, eternal Father, Spirit, Word.
Praise to the Lord of my salvation; salvation is of Christ the Lord.

I bind this day to me for ever, by power of faith, Christ's
    incarnation,
His baptism in Jordan river, his death on cross for my salvation;
His bursting from the spiced tomb, his riding up the heavenly
    way,
His coming at the day of doom, I bind unto myself today.

I bind unto myself today the virtues of the star-lit heaven,
The glorious sun's life-giving ray, the whiteness of the moon
    at even,
The flashing of the lightning free, the whirling wind's
    tempestuous shocks,
The stable earth, the deep salt sea around the old eternal rocks.

I bind unto myself today the power of God to hold and lead,
His eye to watch, his might to stay, his ear to hearken to my
 need,
The wisdom of my God to teach, his hand to guide, his shield
 to ward,
The word of God to give me speech, his heavenly host to be
 my guard.

Christ be with me, Christ within me, Christ behind me, Christ
 before me,
Christ beside me, Christ to win me, Christ to comfort and
 restore me.
Christ beneath me, Christ above me, Christ in quiet, Christ in
 danger,
Christ in hearts of all that love me, Christ in mouth of friend
 and stranger.

I bind unto myself this day the strong name of the Trinity;
By invocation of the same, the three in one and one in three.
Of whom all nature hath creation, eternal Father, Spirit, Word.
Praise to the Lord of my salvation; salvation is of Christ the
 Lord.

If Christians today can learn once more the glory and truth of which
a hymn like that speaks, we will have begun to be the people God is
calling us to be for the world today.

The choice before us must therefore be made clear. You either
embrace this God, this God who is both three and one, or you
embrace idols. The first way is the way to life, to the enhancement
and ultimate affirmation of the humanness that reflects the creator
himself. The second way is the way to ruin, to the ultimate destruction and dehumanization, at every social and personal level, of that
image. This is not dualistic. It simply takes seriously the difference
between good and evil, between the true God and the false gods.

What then is our gospel? It is the announcement, made in the
power of the Spirit, that the crucified and risen Jesus is Lord. This
announcement constitutes a summons to all people to discover the
true fulfilment of every human aspiration and every human dream,
by the paradoxical route of taking up the cross and following Jesus.

This will mean giving up the idols which promise the earth, and embracing the God who promises new heavens and a new earth as the true fulfilment of the present creation. It will mean summoning the powers that at present rule the world to give place to the wise and healing rule of Jesus. There should, of course, be no minimizing of the cost involved in worshipping the true God when surrounded on all sides by idolatry. Aspirations and dreams will find themselves put to death before they can rise again. But this gospel calls human beings, individually and corporately, to find, in cross, resurrection and Spirit, the gift of genuine humanness. This is the gospel we are called to believe and announce.

The choice before the church must therefore also be made clear. Are we to compromise with paganism, to assimilate, to water down the distinctive elements of Christian faith in order to make it more palatable? Are we to retreat into dualism, into a private 'spiritual' religion which will assure us of an other-worldly salvation but which will leave the powers of the present world unchallenged by the Jesus who claims their allegiance? Or are we to worship the God who is Father, Son and Spirit, and to find in that worship a renewed courage, a renewed sense of direction, and a renewed hope for the future?

Questions for reflection or group discussion

1 (a) Where, in your view, does the doctrine of the Trinity address and challenge the life of the world today?
   (b) Where do you think the doctrine of the Trinity challenges the life of the *church* today?

2 (a) Why is it so difficult to believe in the Trinity?
   (b) If St Patrick used a shamrock to explain the doctrine of the Trinity, what images would you use, either to a non-believer or to a Christian who had never thought about it?

Epilogue
The prayer of the Trinity

I suggested in Chapter 13 that there might be different sorts of prayer which could be explored by those seeking appropriate paths of spirituality within the modern world. I want, in this brief epilogue, to suggest one form of prayer in particular which seems to me to encapsulate all that I have been trying to say.

A word, first, about the traditions of prayer upon which this form seeks to draw. The Jews, at least as early as Jesus and probably much earlier, used various prayers on a regular basis. One such may well have been that in which, in Isaiah's great vision in chapter 6, the angels were chanting: 'Holy, holy, holy, is the Lord of hosts; the whole earth is full of his glory.' Another, which formed the basis of regular Jewish daily prayer, was the Shema, which starts: 'Hear, O Israel, the Lord our God, the Lord is One; and you shall love the Lord your God with all your heart, with all your soul, and with all your strength' (Deuteronomy 6.4). This might strike us as something of an odd 'prayer'; it looks more like a credal formula followed by a command. (The rest of the Shema, which continues to verse 9, and then adds Deuteronomy 11.13–21 and Numbers 15.37–41, includes still more commands.) But by Jesus' day it had already sunk deep into the consciousness of the Jewish people, not only as a formula to be repeated three times a day but as a badge of loyalty, an agenda to be followed, a statement of faith which set the compass for another day, another hour, another minute of following the true God wherever he might lead. The noble old Rabbi Akiba, one of those who stood against the Emperor Hadrian's anti-Jewish legislation and died horribly at the hands of his torturers, went on reciting the Shema quietly until he could do so no more. Like the angels ceaselessly chanting 'Holy, holy, holy', the Shema had become, for Akiba, as habitual, and as vital, as breathing.

A different tradition is that of the Eastern Orthodox Church, which I mentioned in Chapter 12. There the 'Jesus Prayer' has been rightly popular: 'Lord Jesus Christ, Son of the living God, have mercy on me, a sinner.' (There are variations, but this is perhaps the best known.) This, like the Jewish Shema, is designed to be said over and over again, until it becomes part of the act of breathing, embedding a sense of the love of Jesus deep within the personality. This prayer, again like the Shema, begins with a confession of faith, but here it is a form of address. And instead of commandments to keep, it focuses on the mercy which the living God extends through his Son to all who will seek it. This prayer has been much beloved by many in the Orthodox and other traditions, who have found that when they did not know what else to pray this prayer would rise, by habit, to their mind and heart, providing a vehicle and focus for whatever concern they wished to bring into the Father's presence.

I have a great admiration for this tradition, but I have always felt a certain uneasiness about it. For a start, it seems to me inadequate to address Jesus only. The Orthodox, of course, have cherished the Trinitarian faith, and it has stood them in good stead over the course of many difficult years. It is true that the prayer contains an implicit doctrine of the Trinity: Jesus is invoked as the Son of the living God, and Christians believe that prayer addressed to this God is itself called forth by the Spirit. But the prayer does not seem to me to embody a fully Trinitarian theology as clearly as it might. In addition, although people more familiar than I with the use of this prayer have spoken of its unfolding to embrace the whole world, in its actual words it is focused very clearly on the person praying, as an individual. Vital though that is, as the private core of the Christian faith without which all else is more or less worthless, it seems to me urgent that our praying should also reflect, more explicitly, the wider concerns with which we have been dealing.

I therefore suggest that we might use a prayer which, though keeping a similar form to that of the Orthodox Jesus Prayer, expands it into a Trinitarian mode:

> Father almighty, maker of heaven and earth:
>> set up your kingdom in our midst.
> Lord Jesus Christ, Son of the living God:
>> have mercy on me, a sinner.
> Holy Spirit, breath of the living God:
>> renew me and all the world.

I would like to say a number of things about this composite prayer by way of explanation. First, as to its emphases. Its opening echoes that of the Lord's Prayer itself, which catches up Israel's longing that her God should bring in his kingdom of justice and peace, and extends these petitions, in the light of Jesus' whole work, to the whole world. Paul does much the same in Ephesians 1, turning older Jewish prayer formulae to new use with a focus on Jesus, meditating on and exulting in God's work in Christ until, with the mention of the Spirit, the Trinitarian picture is complete. In the same way, in the prayer I am suggesting, we invoke the one creator of the whole universe, the one who alone is the source of all things, the one parodied by so much paganism. As we do so, and pray for the coming of his kingdom, we enfold within that prayer our hopes and longings for justice and peace, for the hungry to be satisfied, for the poor to have their needs supplied. This prayer can be used wherever one faces a situation that cries out for God to come and reign as King. In particular, of course, it can be used in what we call evangelism. To present Jesus as the Lord who claims the allegiance of men and women is to seek to bring the kingdom of God to bear on their lives.

By itself, this first clause could become triumphalistic. It could lead us to imagine that we knew exactly what the kingdom would involve, and that we were merely enlisting the creator of the world as the necessary power to achieve the programme we had mapped out. How wrong such prayer would be. Indeed, it is as we pray the heartfelt prayer for the kingdom that we are faced, if we are honest, with the deep realization of our own confusion, inadequacy for the task, rebellion, distortion of God's will, and frank, no-nonsense, old-fashioned sin. It is therefore vital that we keep the middle segment of the prayer much as the Orthodox use it. If, by itself, this part could become self-centred, without it we could become hollow. No Christian can afford to lose the daily and hourly sense of dependence on the free mercy and love of God, mediated through the extraordinary love and grace of Jesus. This prayer, too, can of course be used in the context of particular penitence for particular sin. God knows we will have enough need of it.

But we cannot stop there. Once we have been grasped afresh by the love of God in Jesus, liberating us from our own idolatries so that our work for the kingdom may be free from distortions of our own making, then we must lift our eyes to the world around and see the new work that awaits us. Faced with this, we can and must pray to the Spirit, as Ezekiel was commanded to call for the wind that would come and make the dry bones live. We must pray to the Spirit who alone can give life not only to us but to all the world. And with that prayer we are praying at least three things. We are praying that we ourselves may be healed and renewed, in and from the depths of our own beings, with a healing that will culminate in the resurrection, but which may be anticipated in all kinds of ways during the present life. We are praying, secondly, that others may come to abandon their idolatries and find the truth about the world and its creator in worshipping the God revealed in Jesus. And we are praying, as we must, that the whole creation, non-human as well as human, may find the full rejuvenated life for which it was made. We are praying, that is, for the final coming of the kingdom, only this time seen in terms of the living God flooding his creation, by his Spirit, so that it becomes as a whole what the temple in Jerusalem was supposed to be: the place where he is present, where he is worshipped, where he meets his human creatures in love and grace, the place from which there flow rivers of living and healing water. This is the reality, glimpsed in hope in the gospel, which is parodied in pagan pantheism.

Second, a word about the use of this prayer as a whole. Obviously anyone is free to use it as he or she wishes, but two ways in particular have commended themselves to me.

The first is its use within a litany. The first line of each part can be used as a versicle, and the second as a response. Put together, the three sections cover so many of the areas that the church should be praying for that it would make sense to group different areas of petition under the three heads, repeating each phrase as often as necessary to effect a good rhythm and balance in the whole. The singular 'me' in the second and third clauses could of course become 'us'. And the prayer, thus used, could include praise and confession as well as petition. There are many possibilities here which could be explored, which could help a congregation to turn the concerns of the present book into serious corporate prayer.

The second relates to more personal use. I have spoken of the way in which, in the Jewish and Orthodox traditions, some prayers have become, as it were, embedded in the personality by constant use. I appreciate that some Christians might initially be alarmed by this, for reasons discussed in Chapter 13. Personally, I can see no reason for anxiety, and every reason for welcoming such a practice. If the angels constantly repeat their 'Holy, holy, holy', I cannot see why Christians should not repeat words about the threefold and glorious God. It is *vain* repetitions that we are called to forswear. I suggest that, for some Christians at least, a prayer such as the one I have suggested can become, by constant repetition, the very centre of their human existence.

Most humans, most of the time, have comparatively empty minds, which fill themselves from moment to moment with vague snatches of memory, of odd words and phrases, odd hopes and fears, odd snatches of songs or music. Indeed, it can be a thorough nuisance to have something, as we say, 'in the head' and not to be able to get rid of it. The use of this prayer gently takes this fact about our humanness, this habit of the mind to be continually murmuring on to itself, and woos it with the gospel. It takes responsibility for the times when the mind is 'in neutral'. It replaces the casual, irrelevant, involuntary mental chatter with a quiet, glad repetition of words whose content is incalculably challenging and at the same time incalculably consoling.

Such a manner of praying is not acquired overnight. Indeed, for many people, such a habit might well be inappropriate. For such, there will be other prayers, or other methods of praying this one. But it could, I suspect, be of help to many more than have at present tried anything of the sort. Paul, after all, tells us to 'pray constantly', and though he may simply have meant 'morning, noon and night', the regular times of Jewish prayer, he may also have had in mind the sort of praying I am describing.

The important thing is to start. Perhaps the best way is to use the phrases one at a time: either the first during the morning, the second during the afternoon, and the third during the evening; or possibly the first one day, the second the next, and the third the next. There are no rules. Having begun, perhaps during a regular time of prayer, one can return to the prayer, quietly drawing strength from God in the process, during the busyness and the idleness of the time that follows. Gradually, if we persevere, we shall discover that the prayer rises unbidden to the mind and the heart. It has become part of who we are. And the potential results of such a gradual and quiet change are incalculable, both for oneself, for the church, and for the world.

Such prayer, I suggest, is one way in which all that I have said in this book can become part of the individual Christian life, and part of the praying life of the church. It is vital that the practical tasks I have outlined should not lose their home base in the personal love of the worshipper for the Triune God. That, after all, was the basic command to the people of God who were called to be the light of the world. It was reiterated by Jesus himself as a key point in his own teaching (Mark 12.29–34). We are called to hold firm to Trinitarian monotheism in the face of neo-paganism, and thus to become the people through whom the One God makes his love, holiness, healing and justice known in his world. If the love of God is our message, the love of God must also be our breath of life. Prayer such as this can become a means to this end, equipping the church to face the new God-given tasks.